PRASHAD

INDIAN
VEGETARIAN
COOKING

PRASHAD

INDIAN VEGETARIAN COOKING

KAUSHY PATEL

PHOTOGRAPHY BY
CRISTIAN BARNETT

SALT·YARD
BOOK C.

CONTENTS

FOR MY GRANDMA, PREM MA,

*who showed the world her love through her amazing food,
her desire to feed everyone and the gentle, encouraging way she taught
her skills to me all those years ago. She has inspired me and my
cooking throughout my life, and it is as a result of the kitchen magic
she so lovingly shared with me that I now receive so much joy sharing
that magic with others.*

INTRODUCTION

COOKING has been my world from a very early age. Preparing wonderful food is an expression of real love – a lesson I learned from my amazing grandmother before I was even five years old.

Until I was four, I lived with my parents and three siblings in Ganesh Sisodra, a village in Surat, northern India, about ten miles away from my mother's parents, who lived on a large farm in a village called Pardi. My mother, a sociable woman with a strong sense of family and community, was a great cook. There were always a lot of visitors to our home, and her wide social network brought with it important contacts. It was through them that my father was offered an amazing opportunity to start a business in Zambia.

We were all excited, but my grandma was worried too, as my parents would be leaving India and starting again from scratch. Trying to settle in a foreign land with a young family would be difficult, so she suggested that they leave me behind in India with her, since we already had a special bond. This was true, but nevertheless I was devastated when my mother agreed. I cried for weeks after my family had left and I had moved to Pardi to live with my grandparents.

As it turned out, the next ten years would be the best of my childhood. I missed the rest of my family, obviously, but my grandma made me feel immensely loved, and I soon settled into her wonderful world. She was the most generous and loving person I have ever known, and her enthusiasm for life, food and laughter are still with me today. She believed in cooking with love, and she passionately loved to cook.

And she was *always* cooking – whether for the family or for the hundred or so workers on the farm. She would get up at the crack of dawn to pick vegetables and prepare ingredients for the 'big cook' – making enormous pots of food for the workers before they started their day. I was fascinated by this, quickly got involved and found that I loved to cook. She was thrilled by my desire to learn and carefully taught me until, at the age of seven, I took over the responsibility of cooking for the family while she cooked for the workers.

Before school I would get up early to make the family meal, all the while watching my grandma cooking in the big pots. At the same time she would watch my progress, complimenting me when I succeeded and gently teaching me when I needed help. She impressed on me that the quality of the ingredients and the freshness of the vegetables were all part of the magic – the same magic that we still cook up in Prashad's kitchens – and advised me never to cut corners and always to cook from the heart. When I was fourteen, my mother arranged for me to become engaged to her best friend's son – my soulmate, Mohan. I was to move to England to start my new life, and stay with my uncle in Loughborough (cooking and keeping house for him) while I settled in.

Leaving my grandmother was incredibly hard, but she told me she believed in me and that this was my opportunity to shine. So it was that I landed at Manchester airport in October 1966, not speaking a word of English, still tearful but warmed by her encouragement and blessing. I couldn't believe how cold and dark England was, and how early the sun set! I wasn't convinced that it was the place for me, but I knew that I couldn't disappoint my grandma, so I set out to overcome every obstacle and be a success.

Life was very challenging and not knowing the language was a major hurdle, but I started work in a needle factory as a machine operator and soon discovered plenty of other Indians working there. I picked up English as I went along and gradually things became easier. In 1968 Mohan came to England and we married and moved up to Bradford. I was very shy, but in marriage I found stability and security. With my charming, loving husband by my side, I knew I need never worry or be alone.

The Indian community in Bradford was just developing, and we soon got into a routine of having regular get-togethers with a handful of other young couples from the same part of India, each of us cooking our favourite meals. I loved cooking in my home for my growing family, and welcomed special occasions when I could lay on great feasts. There was scarcely a weekend when we didn't have guests to feed, and my kitchen was fast becoming my world.

Mohan is a fantastic mechanic and had steadily built up a reputable garage business, but by the early 1990s he wanted to try something different. So when he came home one evening in 1992 with a huge grin and told me that the University of Bradford had issued a compulsory purchase order to buy the garage, I knew that the exciting opportunity he had been waiting for had arrived. Knowing that cooking was my lifelong passion, he asked whether I fancied trying the food business. A family friend was selling his launderette, which my mechanical genius husband could run, and attached was a small Indian vegetarian deli from which I could sell my food ... what could be better? My eldest son, Bobby, was studying for his marketing degree at the time, so we asked him to come up with a

name, and his suggestion of Prashad, meaning blessed food, seemed the perfect choice.

Mohan and I were determined that Prashad would have the same quality ethos that my grandma had instilled in me, with no corners cut. He got busy sorting out the building structure and launderette, and I got busy cooking. The more I cooked, the closer I felt to my grandma. Everything I was doing reminded me of her and the recipes she had taught me – even the pot sizes at Prashad were nearly as big as the ones she used for her 'big cook'! I was fulfilling my potential, using the skills she had taught me, cooking her food and making it my own. My food was bringing happiness to me and to many others, and my world started to sing.

The deli was packed with my specialities – Bombay mixes, *dhokra*, *samosas*, spring rolls, *kamree*, *handvo*, *pethis*, vegetable *pakoras* and Indian sweets. Everything you would expect in a Gujarati home could now be bought at Prashad. The business grew, and soon we were being asked to cater for weddings with up to 2,000 guests. Suddenly it was as if I was back in Pardi, cooking for the entire farm with my grandma! We would get up early to prepare the wedding food, then Mohan would head out to deliver it and I would stay in the kitchen to cook for the deli. Once the doors opened for business, I would spend the day talking with customers and selling my food.

As the years went by and the businesses thrived, Bobby noticed that our customers were looking for something more – somewhere they could come to enjoy a whole meal. We were understandably nervous: Mohan and I knew very little about running a restaurant. However,

with a little gentle persuasion from Bobby and my daughter Hina, we introduced some tables and chairs into the deli to see how things went. At around the same time there was a local cooking competition. I was encouraged to enter and decided to give it a go. To my enormous delight, I won! Restaurant critics came to eat in our deli-café and wrote wonderful things about our food. Prashad's reputation as a restaurant started to grow.

Then one afternoon in April 2010, Bobby came bounding into the kitchen shouting, 'Gordon Ramsay is coming to Prashad!' The TV company had called to say that we were close to being selected for the Best Restaurant series. We were excited and worried at the same time. Would Gordon think we were good enough, or should we be doing things differently?

Mohan was the voice of reason: he told us to stop panicking and just do what we had been doing for years – after all, that was why Gordon was coming. So we made a promise that during the show it would be business as normal … and that's what got us to the national restaurant competition finals, shown to millions of viewers and judged by a talented, high-powered TV chef.

Mohan and I are incredibly proud of all our children, and that includes our fourth 'baby', Prashad. We are so happy that we can showcase Gujarati culture in our cuisine and our family ethos – we live together, work together and were thrilled to share our world through the competition.

The restaurant's popularity surged and as a result the deli had to close. It was a sad day for me, but since then many wonderful opportunities have opened up, many of them thanks to Gordon. He has been so generous, helping us in so many ways, including arranging for my daughter-in-law Minal to train at his restaurant Petrus and encouraging me to write this book. We can never thank him enough.

Cooking is a gift that is within everyone's reach. Just remember four simple rules:

1. **Fresh and fantastic**: This is my mantra. Always buy the freshest, best quality ingredients that you can afford. You will taste the difference.

2. **Prepare**: Take the stress out of cooking by preparing your ingredients and getting everything ready in advance.

3. **Relax**: Take time to enjoy your cooking and don't put yourself under pressure to be perfect. No one is a great cook from birth, but by learning from others (and plenty of trial and error) you can create food that is a pleasure to cook and eat.

4. **Cook with love**: My grandma taught me that attitude can affect your food and that love is the most important ingredient, so think beautiful thoughts while you cook!

We Gujaratis use our hands – combining spices, kneading doughs, working in *masalas* – to put all our energy and love into our food. We eat with our hands, too, so we can pick up all that cooked-in love. And we always cook a little more than we need, so that we can invite any unexpected guests to share our meal. If no unexpected guests arrive, the extra food simply gives us an opportunity to share with our neighbours – we call this *vakti vevar* and it helps create great community bonds.

Modern life can be hectic, and one of the first things to suffer is often the sense of community and family. But you can restore the balance with something as simple as a shared meal or a chat over a cup of sweet ginger tea. Food can be so much more than just something to fill you up, and cooking can be so much more than just getting food to the table. The pleasure and sense of achievement in making wonderful meals for yourself, your family or your friends can bring a glow to the face and a smile to the heart.

Throughout my life, I have been blessed to meet (and feed) the most amazing people, and to introduce them to the world of spices, flavours, colours and kitchen magic that I grew up with. Now it's your turn – welcome to my world! Whether you have years of experience in cooking Indian food or are a complete novice, I hope you will enjoy exploring and experimenting with making beautiful, fragrant food through my recipes. Most of all, I hope this book will bring as much joy to you and everyone you cook for (or buy this book for!) as my cooking has brought to me.

 *Kaushy* SEPTEMBER 2012

Kaushy's kitchen
Kaushy's spice tin and seasonings

• • • • • • • • • • • • • • • • • •

Asafetida / asafoetida (*hing*)
Also known as 'devil's dung', due to its pungent, sulphurous scent. The fine yellow powder (which is actually powdered resin) is generally fried in very small quantities when making spiced oils to be used in *dhal* and other dishes to add a savoury flavour. Store in an airtight container – vital to contain the smell. Widely believed to counter flatulence, making it the perfect partner for pulses!

Indian bay leaves (*tej patta*)
Paler than European bay leaves, with a yellow-khaki colour and a straighter edge, these leaves of the Indian cassia tree are used to add a spicy aroma to *chole* (page 132) and rice dishes. Remove from the dish before serving.

Cardamom (*elchi* or *elaichi*)
Available as green, white (bleached) or black/brown pods or as a dried ground spice. I prefer to dry-roast and grind the seeds in a coffee grinder or using a pestle and mortar shortly

before cooking for the freshest flavour. Green cardamom is the most widely used in Indian cooking (I use green cardamom pods and their seeds for all the recipes in this book), and its black seeds are used as a digestive aid and breath freshener. Brown cardamom is used in savoury dishes and in *garam masala*. Store pods away from light and moisture in a jar or airtight tin.

Carom (*ajmo*, *ajwain* or *ajowan*)
Also known as 'Bishop's weed'. The small, curved grey-green seeds resemble celery seeds or tiny cumin seeds. Usually tempered by cooking with other ingredients, eaten raw the seeds are bitter and hot enough to numb the mouth. Thought to calm flatulence and other gastric complaints, carom is often cooked with root vegetables and pulses to aid digestion.

Chilli (*marcha* or *lal/hari mirch*)
There are many different types of chillies (ripe red, unripe green, large, small, fiery, mild) and

they come in many different forms (fresh, dried, flaked, pickled, powdered). I use fresh green chillies from Kenya to make my *masalas*, long green chillies for stuffed chilli *bhajis*, small dried red chillies to add to *tarka* spiced oils, coarse *resam/resham patti* (Kashmiri red chilli powder) from northern India for my pickles to give them a sweeter, less fiery warmth, and medium red chilli powder pretty much everywhere else that a chilli kick is called for.

Cinnamon (*taaj* or *dalchini*)

This spice is made from the bark of the cinnamon tree. It is widely used in main dishes, rice dishes, puddings and sweets, and is believed to help control blood sugar levels. The warm, sweet flavour of cinnamon starts to fade from the sticks after a month or two, so buy it in relatively small amounts to keep the flavour fresh and bright.

Cloves (*lerving* or *laung*)

This small, dark-brown, woody spice is made from dried unopened clove flowerbuds. Often used whole to flavour dishes during cooking and removed before serving, it is also available in powdered form. The oil has anaesthetic qualities, hence its traditional use as a toothache remedy.

Coriander (*dhania* or *dhanna*)

Can be used as a green-leaved herb, in seed form or as a dried ground spice (you get a better flavour if you dry-roast and grind the seeds yourself in a coffee grinder or using a pestle and mortar when needed). When buying seeds, look for light green oval ones. Fresh coriander leaves are sprinkled on many of my dishes shortly before resting or serving, while the spice tends to feature in main dishes, rice dishes and pickles.

Cumin (*jeeru*, *jeera* or *zeera*)

Can be bought as whole seeds or ground spice (for the best flavour, I prefer to dry-roast and grind the seeds shortly before using). The most common cumin seeds are pale green or brown, with a warm, slightly bitter taste; however, you can also find smaller, sweeter black cumin seeds (*kala jeera*). Both types are purported to cure digestive complaints. Ground cumin is often mixed with ground coriander seeds to make *dhania-jeera*.

Curry leaves (*limri*, *kari* or *khadi patta*)

Used fresh or dried, these 'sweet neem' leaves add a pungent aroma and a hint of sweetness to savoury dishes, including delicious southern Indian *kopru* (curry leaf and coconut dip, page 214). They are generally added to spiced oil (*tarka*) rather than cooked directly with other ingredients. Do take care when adding fresh leaves to hot oil, as the moisture in them makes them sizzle and spit. It is a matter of personal choice whether you eat the cooked leaves or not.

Fenugreek (*methi*)

Available as a green-leaved herb (fresh or dried), seeds or crushed spice (*bardho/bardo*). For the best results, roast and crush the seeds yourself when needed. The slightly bitter, aromatic leaves are a central component in many Indian dishes and go beautifully in relishes, flatbreads and in my *methi ni bhaji na bhajia* fritters (page 34). The seeds, which are thought to improve digestion, have a strong curry-like flavour and can be added to spiced oils or directly with other ingredients.

Garam masala

Literally 'hot mixture', this spice blend is used in many dishes and most Indian households will have their own recipe. My secret mixture contains eighteen spices, which are slow-baked for 3 days before being stone-milled. *Garam masala* generally includes roasted ground cinnamon, cardamom, cloves, black cumin, nutmeg and peppercorns, but if you don't fancy making your own, it can also be bought ready-made.

Garlic (*lasan* or *lahsun*)

In recent years, garlic has been hailed as a wonder-food, with antifungal and antiviral properties and beneficial effects on everything from blood pressure to acne. It plays a vital role in Indian cuisine, except during periods of fasting, when our dishes need to be onion and garlic free. I soak garlic cloves in warm water for 5 minutes before I need them, as I find it makes them easier to peel.

Ginger (*adhu* or *adrak*)

Another staple of Indian cooking, ginger is available as a fresh root or dried spice, and lends its heat and warmth to savoury dishes and sweet treats alike. Ginger infusions have long been used to treat sore throats and nausea, and a cup or two of sweet *adhu vari chai* (ginger tea, page 228) always cheers me up. Look for firm roots with no wrinkles or spots, and store any unused ones in the fridge for up to a couple of weeks.

Mustard seeds (*rai*)

There are three main varieties: black, brown and yellow/white, available as whole or split seeds, paste or powdered spice. I use the small brown mustard seeds to bring heat and flavour to spiced oils, and the split yellow seeds (*rai bhardo/bardo* or *rai na kuria*) in pickles, as they are a wonderful preservative. When added to hot oil, brown mustard seeds start to pop as they cook, making it easy to tell that they are working their magic.

Pepper (*mari* or *kali mirch*)

You can buy sharp white, mild green, hot black or fruity pink peppercorns (although the pink ones aren't actually from the pepper plant at all), and pepper is also widely available as a dried ground spice. I use freshly ground black peppercorns in my cooking, as I find that they work best with the other spices – if possible, take the time to grind them freshly for the best aroma and flavour.

Rock salt or black salt
(*kala namak* or *saindhav*)
Mined from quarries rather than harvested from the sea, rock salt has a colour (pink or grey), flavour and aroma all its own. It is somehow less salty than sea salt and is permissible for use in fasting dishes like *ferar bataka* (page 115). You can buy it in powdered form or in crystals to crush at home

Tamarind (*imli* or *amli*)
The name comes from the Arabic '*tamar hindi*', meaning Indian date, which it slightly resembles in taste. I find that pressed block tamarind, consisting of ripe tamarind pod pulp (with the shell and most of the seeds removed), provides a better flavour than concentrated paste. It is used to make tamarind water, which adds a sweet-sour note to dishes (just soak the pulp in warm water for 5 minutes, then sieve). Tamarind is also an ingredient in Worcestershire and HP sauce.

Turmeric (*hardar* or *haldi*)
Often used in Indian wedding and religious ceremonies for cleansing and to bring success. Available as a dried powdered yellow spice with a peppery, earthy flavour and mustardy smell, or a fresh root with golden-orange flesh. Known in medieval Europe as 'Indian saffron' and used to dye fabric, it will stain your hands and clothes yellow if you're not careful. Unpeeled fresh turmeric keeps for up to 3 weeks in the fridge. Avoid cooking it with green vegetables, as it turns them grey.

White turmeric
(*amba haldi* or *amb halad*)
Also known as *zedoary* or 'mango ginger', this closely resembles root ginger. It is less common than turmeric, has a less subtle flavour (like bitter ginger) and can be difficult to find outside India and Indonesia. It adds flavour and colour to dishes but beware the staining effect of the orange juice on hands and clothes too.

Kaushy's ingredients and utensils

. . . .

AGAR AGAR
Vegetarian gelatin substitute derived from algae, also known as kanten, China grass, Japanese moss or Bengal isinglass. It has no scent and a neutral flavour, making it ideal as a base for flavoured jellies and sweets, or for making clear vermicelli to use in *faludha* (page 227). Can also be used as a thickening agent.

BASIL SEEDS, SUBJA, TUK MARIA OR TUK MALANGA
These small black seeds swell when soaked in water, developing a slippery pale grey outer coating over the crunchy central seed. Thought to aid rehydration, they give a deliciously slippery texture in *faludha* (page 227) and can also be used to garnish puddings.

BASMATI RICE
Long-grained rice from northern India with a nutty flavour and fragrant aroma.

Wash thoroughly but gently before cooking to remove the starchy coating, taking care not to break the grains.

BHAGAR OR VAGARIU PAN
Small frying pan used for preparing spiced oils in Gujarati cooking.

BESAN
Gram or chickpea flour (made from ground *chana dhal*) with a nutty flavour and yellow grainy texture. Used for batters, fritters and porridge and in Indian sweets.

BHINDA
Okra, also known as 'ladies' fingers', is part of the mallow family. The fresh green pods can become rather slimy when cooked, so I cut and dry them for 24 hours beforehand to avoid this. The gooey glutinous juice can be used to thicken soups and sauces.

Also known as calabash or long melon.
Immature gourds are used for cooking,
mature ones are dried and used as containers,
originally as bottles for carrying water
(hence the name). Always try a small piece of
gourd while you are grating it, and don't
use it if it tastes bitter, as bitter gourd juice
can sometimes cause stomach problems.

BROKEN RICE

Rice, often basmati, which has broken or
cracked during harvesting or drying. Starchier
(and cheaper) than whole rice grains. Used
for sticky rice and porridge dishes, as well as
my *masala dosa* batter (page 145).

BROKEN WHEAT, CRACKED WHEAT OR LAPSI

Used in Indian cooking for puddings,
snacks and porridge dishes, to which it
brings a chewy texture and slightly nutty
flavour. It is made from raw unrefined
wheat and needs to be fully cooked (not to
be confused with bulgur wheat, which is
steamed and dried before cracking,
so needs very little further cooking).
Easy to digest.

CHANA DHAL

Bengal gram *dhal*/split skinned black chickpeas.
Renowned for causing flatulence, so it is often
cooked with asafetida or carom to counteract this!

CHAPATTI FLOUR, ATTA OR LOHT

Wheat flour, used for making *rotlis* and
other breads. Available as refined white flour
or wholewheat brown flour.

CHIKOO, SAPODILLA OR CHICO FRUIT

Also known in India as the *sapota* or 'tree potato',
the fruit looks rather like a smooth tennis-ball-
sized potato. The flavour and texture of the
yellowy-brown flesh are similar to that of a very
ripe pear, but with malty caramel tones. It contains
a small number of hooked black seeds that need
to be removed, as they can stick in the throat.

CORNFLOUR, CORN/MAIZE FLOUR, MAKAI NO LOHT OR MAKKI KA ATTA

Fine flour made from ground maize
or sweetcorn kernels. Typically used in batters
and doughs.

DESI CHANA, KALA CHANA OR BENGAL GRAM

Black or brown chickpeas. They are smaller
and darker than *kabuli* chickpeas, have a

rougher skin and are probably the ancestor of the cultivated chickpea. They have a nutty flavour and are higher in fibre than conventional chickpeas, making them more suitable for people with blood sugar issues. If using dried *desi chana*, soak for 8 hours before cooking.

DOSA

A thin crispy pancake, originating from southern India and made with a fermented ground rice and *urad dhal*.

FRUIT SALTS

Effervescent fruit salts (e.g. Eno), traditionally used to relieve indigestion, can also be used as a leavening agent in yeast-free breads. My grandmother always used fruit salts in this way. If you don't have any, substitute the same quantity of baking powder (or use bicarbonate of soda in recipes where there are acidic ingredients, e.g. lemon juice or yoghurt).

GHUVAR OR GREEN CLUSTER BEAN

Paler, flatter and more fibrous than French and string beans (which can be used as a substitute), cluster beans are also slightly bitter. As a result, many *ghuvar* dishes, including mine, contain a little sugar to balance the flavours.

GHEE

Clarified butter, much used in traditional Indian cooking either as an ingredient (e.g. in *bhakri ladoo*, page 243) or to drizzle over dishes when serving (e.g. over *velmi*, page 182, my favourite bread). Traditionally made with cow or buffalo milk butter (the latter has a higher fat content).

GHILORA OR IVY GOURD

Also known by a variety of other names including 'baby watermelon', 'little gourd' and 'gentleman's toes'! Grown on a vine, similar to its cousin the cucumber. Try to buy slim gourds, rather than overripe plump ones whose flesh has turned red.

GREEN MANGO

Young unripe mango, used as a sour fruit in chutney, pickles and relishes. The stone should still be soft enough to cut through.

HANDI

A deep, round, thick-bottomed cooking pot, narrower at the top than in the middle. Covered and placed directly on charcoals, it is used to cook dishes that need lengthy simmering to bring out their full flavour.

INDIAN LEMON

Smaller and rounder than Mediterranean lemons, Indian lemons also have a much thinner skin. Limes can be used as a substitute.

JAGGERY, GHOR OR GUR

Unrefined dehydrated cane sugar juice. Used to add sweetness to curries, breads, puddings and sweets, it has a slightly caramel-like sweet flavour. If you can't get hold of any, use soft brown or demerara sugar instead.

JUVAR, JOWAR, SORGHUM FLOUR OR MILO FLOUR

Gluten-free flour made from ground sorghum grain kernels. Suitable for coeliacs and others with gluten intolerance. Nutritionally similar to corn flour, although higher in protein and fat, it has long been used in India to make pancakes and flatbreads, including *juvar na rotla* (page 173).

KABULI CHANA

White chickpeas, used for making *chole* (page 132). Can be bought either dried (in which case soak for at least 8 hours before cooking) or tinned in water or brine.

MASOOR DHAL

Whole or split husked red lentils. The husk is a speckled greeny-brown while the centre is pinky-orange. Split *masoor dhal* is fast-cooking and delicately nutty in flavour.

MOMRA, KURMURA OR MAMRA

Puffed rice – a vital ingredient in many snack and streetfood dishes. Store in an airtight container and try to use up quickly once you have opened the packet, as it will quickly soften and lose its crispness once exposed to the air.

MUNG OR MOONG

Whole mung beans. They have a khaki-green husk and are therefore also known as green gram. Need to be soaked in advance to reduce cooking time.

MUNG OR MOONG DHAL

Yellow split, husked mung beans. They are easy to cook (no need to soak) and easy to digest too, so are often served to children, the elderly and the infirm – e.g. in *mung dhal kichdi* (page 167).

PANEER
Fresh, unsalted Indian white cheese, traditionally made at home but now widely available in supermarkets and Indian stores. Firm-textured and often griddled or fried.

PATRA
Leaves of the colocasia plant, also known as the elephant-ear plant or cocoyam. The green arrowhead-shaped leaves can grow up to 150cm long, although for cooking you usually need either small (10 x 15cm) or medium (20 x 20cm) leaves. Dishes like *bafela patra* (page 57), using the stuffed leaves, are a Gujarati speciality.

PAUWA, PAWA or POHA
Flattened, beaten or pounded parboiled rice, often used in *chaat* dishes or as a form of Indian fast food. *Pauwa* flakes are available in differing thicknesses, from thick to fine, depending on the weight of the rollers used to flatten it.

RATALU, PURPLE YAM or VIOLET YAM
A cylindrical root with a thick uneven skin, requiring substantial peeling to reach the

slightly sticky, sweet purple interior. My favourite vegetable!

RICE FLOUR
Slightly grainy white flour made from ground washed dried rice. I tend to use it in doughs and batters, but it can also be used to thicken sauces.

SEMOLINA, SOJI or SOOJI
Available as coarse, medium or fine, this pale yellow processed durum wheat flour is used in sweet and savoury dishes.

SEV
Crispy Indian vermicelli noodles made

from chickpea flour, used in *chaat* dishes, as a garnish or as a snack.

SEV MOMRA OR SEV MAMRA
Indian vermicelli combined with puffed rice. A popular snack food.

TARKA OR TADKA
Spiced oil, stirred into *dhal* or other dishes towards the end of the cooking process to bring the spices to life. Traditionally prepared by heating *ghee* and spices together in a long-handled ladle.

TAWA
Shallow metal frying pan or griddle.

THALI
Indian multi-compartment dinner plate (traditionally made of steel) which allows a variety of different dishes including rice, pickles and sauces to be contained separately.
These days also used to describe a full Gujarati meal consisting of *rotli*, *dhal*, *bhaat* and *shaak* (bread, lentils, rice and vegetables).

TUVAR DHAL, TOOR DHAL OR ARHAR DHAL
Split husked dried pigeon peas or yellow lentils

(also known as congo or gungo peas). The denser texture means that this requires longer soaking and/or longer cooking times than other *dhals*. Any oily coating should be thoroughly rubbed and rinsed away before cooking.

URAD DHAL, URID DHAL OR BLACK GRAM
With their black husk and white centre, these are called 'black lentils' when whole and 'white lentils' when split and husked.

VALOR OR HYACINTH BEANS
Also known as val bean, valore bean or Indian bean, the purple pods and fragrant flowers are very attractive. I recommend that whenever possible you use fresh hyacinth beans (bought in the pod, which you also cook and eat), as you need to be very careful using the dried beans – they require prolonged boiling to remove toxins.

WHITE POPPY SEEDS, KHASKAHAS OR KHUSKHUS
Like European black or grey poppy seeds and Turkish brown poppy seeds, Indian white poppy seeds can be used in sweet and savoury dishes either as an ingredient or a garnish. They add thickness and texture as well as a subtle nutty flavour.

PRACTICAL POINTS, TOP TIPS AND HOW TO ...

- All my recipes are marked with the following notations to help you to choose the right one for you.

V – VEGAN WF – WHEAT-FREE

OG – ONION- & GARLIC-FREE N – NUT-FREE

HO – HEALTHY OPTION

- My local Indian stores are full of great ingredients, but I realize that not everyone has a local Indian store. As a result, when my recipe calls for an unusual ingredient, I generally try to suggest an alternative in case you can't get hold of it, as there is almost always something else you can use instead. This advice applies throughout my recipes: don't feel that you always have to follow them to the letter – if it isn't possible to find an ingredient you need or if there's something you'd rather change, improvise and try an alternative (it's your meal after all). Much of the process of great cooking is trial and error – sometimes we make mistakes, and sometimes we make magic.

PREPARATION

- Onions, garlic, carrots, etc., in ingredients lists are all peeled unless the recipe states otherwise.

- Sometimes vegetables (usually potatoes and, in one recipe, unripe bananas) are washed but not peeled because they are to be cooked in their skins – but don't worry, the recipe will make it clear when the skin is left on and when it is peeled off.

- Where the ingredient is potentially unfamiliar to you (e.g. bottle gourd, purple yam, turmeric root, etc.), I have included preparation instructions in the recipe.

- Sweet peppers are always deseeded, but most of the fresh chillies have their seeds left in, as I like the flavour and heat that the seeds add.

- When using fresh coriander, I trim away up to 4cm of the stalks.

- I tend to use fresh grated coconut in my cooking, but if you can't find any, you can generally substitute unsweetened desiccated coconut, rehydrated in warm water and drained.

- If the recipe doesn't call for a specific sugar, feel free to use whichever type you have to hand – I tend to use granulated white sugar.

- The oil for cooking will always be sunflower oil unless otherwise specified.

• I use plain live set yoghurt throughout my recipes because of its tangy taste and the creamy consistency even when whisked – it holds its structure better than runny yoghurt.

• I find that soaking garlic cloves in warm water for 5 minutes makes them easier to peel.

• The amount of chilli in my recipes is expressed as a range, so that you can decide how much to use depending on how hot you like your food. In the restaurant and in my home cooking, I use the higher number of chillies, but that's because I eat chillies every day.

• Chillies vary in potency depending on where they come from and the season, so try them out, then vary the quantity according to taste. Remember, you can always add more chilli – it's a lot harder to remove!

• If you are not used to chilli heat, you may wish to deseed fresh chillies, then soak them in cold salt water for a few minutes before chopping.

• And do take care to wear gloves when cutting chillies, so that you don't risk rubbing the juice into your eyes or lips by mistake.

• The longer you rest a dish, the more the flavours will develop and mellow, and the less heat there should be from the chillies. Many of my main dishes can be rested for hours (or even made the day before) and then reheated before serving.

• Whenever possible cook with vine tomatoes, as they taste more like home-grown tomatoes.

• Washing *dhals* – I do this using my fingertips to remove any oily coating and to make sure they get a thorough clean (the water should run clear by the end). Using my hands also helps me to find and remove any small stones that may have crept in when the pulses were being sorted or packaged.

• Rinsing rice several times before cooking washes away enough starch to make sure your rice will be fluffy and loose when cooked, but do take care not to break the grains, as this will make it more (rather than less) starchy.

• I find that mixing the marinade with my hands helps the combination of spices to come alive.

• Have a go at grinding your own spices, rather than buying them ready-ground – you will find the flavours much more intense. When a recipe calls for ground cardamom seeds, for example, gently crush a few green cardamom pods and extract the little round black seeds. Then grind these in an electric coffee/spice grinder or crush using a pestle and mortar for wonderfully fragrant ground cardamom. Some spices like cumin seeds require roasting before you grind them, but it's very simple to do – see my How To tips box on page 26.

• Sometimes when making *bhajia*, you may have some batter left over. Rather than waste it, cut a potato (washed but not peeled) into 5mm-thick slices, then batter and fry to make crispy *kakra bhajia* (potato fritters, page 39).

• Try not to cook when you are stressed or short of time – cooking should be a pleasure as well as a means to an end. And always think beautiful thoughts while you cook. Not only will it make you feel happier, but it makes your food taste beautiful too!

ROAST CUMIN SEEDS

Dry-roast the cumin seeds in a frying pan over a low heat for about 2 minutes, shaking the pan to toast them evenly, until they start to darken slightly. Set aside to cool, then just before you need to add the spice to your dish, use a pestle and mortar or a blender to crush the seeds finely. A tablespoon of seeds will yield about 4–5 teaspoons of ground cumin.

STOP CHOPPED AUBERGINE OR POTATO FROM OXIDIZING

When cutting aubergines or potatoes in advance, put the pieces into a bowl of water as soon as you've cut them. Drain when you're ready to cook them.

STOP YOUR DHAL PAN FOAMING OVER

Once the *dhal* starts to foam, skim the froth from the top and add a teaspoon of oil to the water to stop it bubbling up.

PREVENT TARKA SPICES FROM BURNING

When making a *tarka* spiced oil, reduce the heat as soon as the seeds start to brown as they will continue to cook in the hot oil.

PICK AND PREPARE FRESH COCONUT

When buying fresh coconuts, look for ones with plenty of water in them (give them a good shake) and no mildew on the 'eyes'. To open, gently crack with a hammer and drain out the coconut water – it makes a delicious refreshing drink. Use the hammer to break open the shell. Prise out the coconut 'meat', use a vegetable peeler to remove the brown skin, then grate. You can freeze any you don't need – frozen grated coconut will keep for up to 3 months.

ADD MOIST INGREDIENTS TO HOT OIL SAFELY

Always reduce the heat before adding anything that contains moisture (e.g. chopped onion or fresh curry leaves) to hot oil, as the water will cause the oil to spit on contact and if it catches you, it can cause nasty burns. Just add, stand well back and enjoy the sizzle!

BALANCE CHILLI-HOT FOOD

Yoghurty dishes and sweet dishes will temper the fire from chillies. Serve a yoghurt dip or mango *lassi* with your meal to cool the taste buds, or try having a little something sweet after a particularly hot mouthful – you'll be amazed at the difference it can make!

STARTERS

STARTERS

★ ★ ★ ★ ★

In traditional Gujarati cooking we don't serve starters, main dishes and desserts separately, one after another, as in many other types of cuisine. Instead all the dishes are placed on the table at the same time – crispy *bhajis* and *pethis* side-by-side with aromatic curries and *dhals*, fluffy rice and steaming flatbreads next to sweet dishes, pickles, dips and cooling *raitu* – creating a glorious feast for the eyes and the stomach. Everyone helps themselves to a little bit of everything, filling the separate compartments of their *thali* plate and creating their own flavour combinations with each mouthful of the sweet, sour, salty and spicy foods.

The practice of serving smaller snacks at the start of the meal really only began in Indian restaurants as a way of providing something for customers to eat while they waited for their main dish. However, it is a practice that we have embraced wholeheartedly, not least because our cooking has so many fantastic dishes that are perfectly suited to being starters.

Some of these – like crispy fenugreek and banana *bhajis*, crunchy vegetable *pakora* and

garlicky-coconut filled *pethis* – are deep-fried, which gives them a fantastic texture and flavour, ideal to eat hot and fresh from the kitchen. Some, like savoury *handvo* (seed-topped lentil cake) and *dhokra* (chickpea cake), are steamed for a beautiful soft sponge-like texture. Others, like our Prashad spring rolls, Gujarati *samosas* and Minal's *hara bara* kebab (pea and cauliflower kebabs), are traditionally fried but can be oven-baked if you prefer, giving a healthier option.

There is wonderful variety in the appearance and texture of these starter dishes too. Crisp golden *bataka vada* (lemon and coriander potato balls) are a delicious contrast to the light and dark green concentric rings and soft texture of sliced *bafela patra* (colocasia leaf rolls). Colourful *paneer tikka* skewers, with their firm griddled cheese and fresh vegetable chunks, look bright and bold against delicate seed-sprinkled *pathudi* (pancake rolls). Last but definitely not least, the rich colours in my favourite starter, *ratalu puri*, and the sweetness of the purple yam combined with firm potato and the spicy peanut and coconut marinade, are guaranteed to make your mouth water!

STARTERS

Methi ni bhaji na bhajia – Fenugreek leaf and banana bhajis

(WF, N)

Versatile fenugreek is used regularly in Indian cooking, as a herb (the leaves), a spice (the seeds) and a vegetable (the leaves and sprouts). This dish (also known as kalva*) reminds me of my grandmother in India – whenever anyone came to visit, she would run into the garden to pick the fresh fenugreek and rustle up this amazing starter in minutes. The addition of the yoghurt makes the* bhajis *lighter and fluffier, but you can leave it out if you prefer.*

SERVES 4

sunflower oil, for frying

Masala

1–2 fresh green chillies, seeds left in
2 cloves of garlic
1cm root ginger, peeled and
  roughly chopped
pinch of salt

Batter

100g fresh fenugreek leaves,
  rinsed and finely chopped
175g chickpea flour
1 teaspoon coarsely ground
  black pepper
1 tablespoon ground coriander
1 teaspoon medium red
  chilli powder
1¼ teaspoons salt
2 tablespoons sugar
1 ripe medium banana, mashed
¼ teaspoon turmeric
1 teaspoon plain live set yoghurt
  (optional)

Crush the chillies, garlic and ginger together with a pinch of salt using a pestle and mortar (or a blender), to make a fine masala paste.

Put all the batter ingredients into a medium bowl, including the yoghurt (if using). Add the masala paste and lightly mix everything together with your hands. Add 50ml of warm water and mix again. Add another 50ml of water and continue to mix until the batter is lovely and smooth.

Heat the frying oil – about 15cm deep – in a large pan over a high heat (or in a deep fat fryer, if you have one). Test the temperature by sprinkling a few small drops of batter into the oil – when it is hot enough, they will float to the surface. Reduce the heat to medium.

Delicately spoon small teaspoonfuls of batter into the oil until the pan (or fryer) is full, then leave to cook for 1 minute, until the *bhajia* are golden brown on top. Gently turn them over to fry the other side for 1 minute more. Make sure they don't overcook – take them out once they are just golden brown and leave them to rest on kitchen paper while you make the next batch. Repeat this process until the batter is used up.

Serve immediately, with *phudino dai* (page 211), ideally accompanied by *wattana* and flower (page 118) or a cup of *adhu vari chai* (page 228).

Bataka bhajia –
Potato fritters with coriander and pepper crunch

(V, WF, N)

I really enjoy the look as well as the taste of these bhajia *– the sprinkling of pepper and spicy citrussy coriander seeds immediately before frying is very attractive and introduces a superb crunch. Just thinking about them makes my mouth water ...*

SERVES 4 (MAKES ABOUT 20)

2 medium red-skinned
  (or other waxy) potatoes
4 tablespoons coriander seeds,
  coarsely crushed
1 tablespoon black peppercorns,
  coarsely ground or crushed
sunflower oil, for frying

Masala

2–5 fresh green chillies, seeds left in
2–4 cloves of garlic
pinch of salt

Batter

200g chickpea flour, sieved
20g rice flour
1¼ teaspoons salt
1 handful of fresh coriander,
  finely chopped

Crush the chillies and garlic together with a pinch of salt using a pestle and mortar (or a blender), to make a fine masala paste.

Put the batter ingredients into a medium bowl. Add 300ml of warm water and the masala paste and mix gently to form a relatively runny batter. Cut the potatoes into 5mm slices. Mix the coriander seeds and pepper in a small bowl.

Heat the frying oil – about 15cm deep – in a large pan over a high heat (or in a deep fat fryer, if you have one). Test the temperature by sprinkling a few drops of batter into the oil – when it is hot enough, they will float to the surface. Reduce the heat to medium.

Put 4 potato slices at a time into the batter, making sure they are fully coated. Take one slice out of the batter and hold it horizontally. Sprinkle the top surface with some of the seed/pepper mix, then carefully place in the oil, sprinkled side uppermost. Repeat with the remaining 3 slices. Some batter droplets may run off into the oil – use a slotted spoon to remove them so that they don't burn. After 3 minutes, turn the slices over and cook for a further 4–5 minutes, until the batter is a crisp golden brown and the seeds are dark brown. Remove from the oil and leave to rest on kitchen paper while you batter and fry the remaining potato slices in batches of 4 at a time.

Serve warm, with *kakadhi raitu* (page 212) or *safarjan wattana* (page 208).

Marcha na bhajia – Stuffed chilli bhajis

(V, WF)

*This is a long-standing favourite at the restaurant. I first created the recipe in the days
of the deli, when my customers wanted something substantial at lunchtime. We used to sell
starters by weight in those days, and I remember my younger son, Mayur, being surprised
at just how heavy these were. The addition of rice flour to the batter helps make these wonderfully
crisp. It is important to boil the potatoes in their skins and peel them after cooking, as this
ensures that they don't absorb too much water. This recipe calls for long chillies, which look like
stretched green peppers. You can find them in Indian food stores, but if you can't get hold of any,
use sweet red Romano peppers instead – you won't get the spicy kick of the long chillies,
but the* bhajia *will still taste delicious.*

SERVES 4

8 medium-sized long green chillies
  (up to 12cm)
sunflower oil, for frying

Masala
1–3 fresh green chillies, seeds left in
1–3 cloves of garlic
pinch of salt

Filling
2 medium red-skinned
  (or other waxy) potatoes
2 handfuls of fresh coriander,
  finely chopped
4 tablespoons sesame seeds
1 teaspoon salt
pinch of turmeric
2 teaspoons sugar
4 tablespoons unsweetened
  desiccated coconut
4 teaspoons lemon juice
1 teaspoon garam masala

First make the masala. Crush the chillies and garlic
together with a pinch of salt using a pestle and mortar
(or a blender), to make a fine paste.

Boil the potatoes in their skins for 40 minutes or so,
until a knife tip will slide in easily, then peel and mash.
Put the mashed potato and the other filling ingredients
into a medium bowl, then add the masala paste and mix
using your hands. Make sure you work all the spices
into the filling, but try not to overwork the mixture or
the potato will become gluey. Set aside.

Put the flours into another medium bowl and add the
salt, chilli powder and 300ml of warm water. Whisk the
batter until it is smooth – don't be tempted to add extra
water, as it is better to have a slightly thicker batter than
one that is too runny.

Trim the long green chilli stems to about 2cm. Cut each
chilli along its length on one side, leaving about 0.5cm
uncut at each end to help keep its shape and contain the
filling. Remove the seeds (I hold the chilli cut side down
and tap with the flat of the knife to knock them out),
then carefully open slightly and spoon some of the filling
into the cavity. Work it in with your thumb, adding more

Batter

200g chickpea flour, sieved
20g rice flour
½ teaspoon salt
½ teaspoon medium red chilli powder

as necessary and wiping off any excess once the chilli is full. Repeat with the rest of the chillies.

Heat the frying oil – about 25cm deep – in a large pan over a high heat (or in a deep fat fryer, if you have one). Test the temperature by sprinkling a few drops of batter into the oil – when it is hot enough, they will float to the surface. Reduce the heat to medium.

Hold one of the chillies by the stem and carefully place it in the batter, spooning the batter over it until thoroughly coated. Gently lower the chilli into the oil, holding the stem until the chilli is almost fully submerged. Repeat until you have up to 4 chillies frying at the same time. Fry for 8–10 minutes, until crisp and golden brown, turning them over every minute or so. Remove from the oil and leave to rest on kitchen paper while you cook the rest of the chillies.

Ideally serve straight away – although they are also delicious served warm – with *safarjan wattana* chutney (page 208).

 KAUSHY'S TOP TIP

Kakra bhajia (POTATO FRITTERS)

Depending on the size of your chillies, you may have some batter left over. Rather than waste it, cut a potato (washed but not peeled) into 5mm slices, then dip them in batter and fry in the same oil to make crispy *kakra bhajia* fritters. Sprinkle the cooked *bhajia* with a little medium red chilli powder and enjoy with plenty of *imli* chutney (page 210) or your favourite dip.

Vegetable pakora –
Spicy cauliflower and cabbage fritters

(WF, N)

*Always a favourite starter, these are best when served hot and crispy, fresh from the fryer.
My son Bobby orders* pakora *whenever he goes to an Indian restaurant, in order to get a quick
idea of the quality of their cooking – if they are crisp on the outside and moist in the middle, he is
generally in for a good meal. Garam masala, which means 'hot mixture', can be shop-bought
or homemade. It may contain a variety of different spices, depending on personal taste and
regional background. The exact recipe for an Indian family's* garam masala *is often a closely
guarded secret, as mine is!*

MAKES 16–20

2–4 fresh green chillies, seeds left in

150g chickpea flour, sieved

1 tablespoon rice flour

1 tablespoon sunflower oil,
  plus more for frying

1½ teaspoons salt

1 tablespoon ground coriander

1 tablespoon plain live set yoghurt

1 handful of fresh coriander,
  finely chopped

½ teaspoon medium red chilli powder

pinch of turmeric

1 teaspoon *garam masala*

1 tablespoon coriander seeds,
  coarsely crushed

1 teaspoon black peppercorns,
  coarsely ground or crushed

½ x 400g tin of peeled plum tomatoes

1 tomato, cut into 1cm chunks

¼ small cauliflower,
  cut into 1cm chunks

¼ small head of white cabbage,
  cut into 1cm chunks

1 small onion, roughly diced

Chop or blend the chillies to a fine paste. Put the flours, green chilli paste, oil, salt, ground coriander, yoghurt, fresh coriander, chilli power, turmeric, *garam masala*, coriander seeds, black pepper, tinned tomatoes and fresh tomato into a large bowl, then add 50ml of warm water and mix well to form a stiff batter. Gently stir in the cauliflower, cabbage and onion pieces, being careful not to break up the cauliflower. Leave to rest for 10 minutes.

Heat the frying oil – about 20cm deep – in a large pan over a high heat (or in a deep fat fryer, if you have one). Test the temperature by sprinkling a few drops of batter into the oil – when it is hot enough, they will float to the surface. Reduce the heat to medium.

Carefully drop tablespoons of the batter into the oil until the pan is full. Leave to cook for 2–3 minutes, until the undersides are golden brown. Gently turn the *pakora* over with a slotted spoon and fry for a further 2–3 minutes. Make sure they don't overcook – take them out once they are just golden brown and leave to rest on kitchen paper while you fry the next batch. Repeat until the batter is used up.

Serve immediately, with *kacha* tomato relish (page 207) and/or *phudino dai* (page 211).

Kandha na bhajia – Onion ring fritters

(V, WF, N)

These onion bhajia *make a lovely little starter. Eat them as soon as they are cooked, as they only remain crisp for a short time.*

SERVES 4

sunflower oil, for frying
3 medium onions

Masala
3–6 fresh green chillies, seeds left in
3–4 cloves of garlic
pinch of salt

Batter
200g chickpea flour
20g rice flour
1¼ teaspoon salt
1 teaspoon black peppercorns,
 coarsely ground or crushed
1 handful of fresh coriander,
 finely chopped
1 teaspoon carom seeds

Crush the chillies and garlic together with a pinch of salt, using a pestle and mortar (or a blender), to make a fine masala paste.

Put the flours, salt, pepper, coriander and carom seeds into a medium bowl, add the masala paste and 300ml of warm water, then lightly but thoroughly mix everything together until you have a slightly runny batter.

Heat the frying oil – about 15cm deep – in a large pan over a high heat (or in a deep fat fryer, if you have one). Test the temperature by sprinkling a few drops of batter into the oil – when it is hot enough, they will float to the surface. Reduce the heat to medium.

Slice the onions into rings about 1cm wide, setting aside the smallest central rings as they will be too small to fry without burning. Put a handful of onion rings into the batter, making sure they are fully covered. (Don't put all the rings into the batter at once, as they will release juice into the batter and make it too runny.)

Delicately place the battered onion rings in the oil and cook for 2 minutes before turning them over. Fry for a further 3–4 minutes, turning every minute or so, until golden brown and crisp. Take care not to overcook them, as they fry quite quickly. Remove the cooked *bhajia* from the oil and leave to rest on kitchen paper while you make the next batch. Repeat until all the onion rings have been used up.

Serve immediately, with *safarjan wattana* chutney (page 208).

VARIATION – RENGHAN BHAJIA (AUBERGINE FRITTERS)

My daughter-in-law Minal introduced *renghan bhajia* to Prashad about four years ago. I was having lunch with my friend Marion and we decided to try them – they were so delicious I couldn't stop talking about them! To make your own, use 2 large aubergines, cut into 1cm wide slices, instead of the onion rings and fry for a couple of minutes, until golden brown.

Gujarati mixed vegetable samosas – Potato, pea and carrot parcels

(V, OG, N)

These stuffed pastry parcels are bursting with flavour. We made baby samosas for my daughter's engagement party, and the guests went wild for them. It was a wonderful day, celebrating (and eating, of course) with more than 500 friends and family. The traditional method of making samosas involves filling and sealing soft dough cones while you hold them in your hand, but there is also a simpler method in which you form the dough parcels around the filling on your work surface. If this is your first attempt at making samosas, you may wish to use the simplified method.

SERVES 6 (MAKES 24)

sunflower oil, for frying
50g plain flour

Filling

1–3 fresh green chillies, seeds left in
150g frozen peas (ideally *petits pois*)
50ml sunflower oil
1 teaspoon cumin seeds
3 medium red-skinned (or other waxy)
  potatoes, cut into 5mm cubes
1 medium carrot, cut into 5mm cubes
1 teaspoon salt
pinch of turmeric
½ teaspoon medium red chilli powder
2 handfuls of fresh coriander,
  finely chopped
½ teaspoon *garam masala*

Dough

300g plain flour
8 teaspoons sunflower oil
4 teaspoons lemon juice
pinch of salt

Crush the chillies into a fine paste using a pestle and mortar (or a blender). Rinse the peas in warm water to start them thawing.

Heat the oil and cumin seeds in a large pan over a medium heat. When the seeds start to turn brown, stir in the potato and carrot cubes, then cover the pan and cook over a low heat for 5 minutes. Stir in the green chilli paste, peas, salt, turmeric, chilli powder and half the chopped coriander, then cover again and cook over a low heat for 10 minutes. Remove from the heat, stir in the *garam masala* and the remaining coriander, and tip on to a large baking tray. Spread the filling over the tray and set aside to cool.

Combine all the dough ingredients in a large bowl, rubbing the oil and lemon juice through the flour and salt, then add 175ml of boiling water and mix with a spoon. Once cool enough to handle, knead until the dough comes together. Smooth a little oil over the surface of the dough, then divide into 12 pieces, forming each one into a ball. Roll the balls into thin discs (roughly 18cm in diameter) on a lightly floured work surface.

Heat a frying pan over a medium heat and dry-fry each dough disc for about 1 minute on each side – this is enough to half-cook them. Stack the half-cooked discs on top of each other on a chopping board. Use a sharp knife to cut the stack of discs in half, then cover the 2 stacks of dough semicircles with a dry tea towel.

Put the flour into a small bowl and slowly add 100ml of warm water, whisking all the time, until the mixture forms a runny, sticky paste for sealing the *samosas*.

TRADITIONAL METHOD: Take one of the dough semicircles and place it on a work surface or chopping board with the cut edge closest to you. Pick up the right-hand corner and fold it up to meet the centre of the curved edge. Dab a little of the flour/water paste along the straight edge that will form the seam of the cone. Lift up the left-hand corner of the dough semicircle and fold it up so that it also meets the centre of the curved edge, slightly overlapping the (now paste-covered) other straight edge. Press the overlapping seam gently to seal. Hold the folded dough in your palm, point facing downwards, and carefully open to form a cone. Spoon 4 teaspoons of filling into the cone until the filling reaches about 1cm or so below the top, taking care not to overfill. Fold the seam side edge of the cone on top of the filling, dab the pastry with paste and stick the other side of the cone on top to seal the *samosa*. Check that the points of the *samosa* are properly sealed, then place seam side down on a baking tray and repeat with the other dough semicircles.

SIMPLIFIED METHOD: Take one of the dough semicircles and place it on a work surface or chopping board with the cut edge closest to you. Dab flour/water paste all around the edges of the semicircle. Spoon 4 teaspoons of filling on to the middle of the dough. Pick up the right-hand corner and fold it up to meet the centre of the curved edge, pressing gently around the outside edge to seal. Lift up the left-hand corner of the dough semicircle and fold it up so that it also meets the centre of the curved edge, slightly overlapping the other straight edge. Press gently around the outside edge and along the overlapping seam to seal in the filling. Check that the points of the *samosa* are properly sealed, then place seam side down on a baking tray and repeat with the other dough semicircles.

Whichever method you use, remember to save a bit of dough when making the last *samosa*, for testing the oil temperature. Heat the frying oil – about 20cm deep – in a large pan over a high heat (or in a deep fat fryer, if you have one). Test the temperature by dropping your little piece of dough into the oil – when it is hot enough, it will float to the surface. Reduce the heat to medium.

Gently lower 4 or 5 *samosas* into the oil, and use a wooden spoon to move them around so that they cook evenly all over. Fry until golden brown and crispy – this should take about 6 minutes or so, depending on the oil temperature. Remove from the oil with a slotted spoon and leave to rest on kitchen paper while you fry the next batch. Repeat until all the *samosas* have been fried.

Serve while hot and crispy, with plenty of *safarjan wattana* chutney (page 208).

VARIATION – BAKED SAMOSAS

If you are looking for a healthier option to deep-frying, you can oven-bake your *samosas*. Preheat the oven to 180°C/160°C fan/gas mark 4 and oil a baking tray. Place the uncooked *samosas* on the tray, brush or spray with oil and cook for 30 minutes, turning after the first 10 minutes to help them crisp up evenly.

Prashad spring rolls

(V, OG)

I remember when I first developed this recipe and started selling spring rolls in our deli. They were one of our fastest-selling starters, with some people buying hundreds at a time! My daughter Hina loves them too – they are the perfect comfort food to eat on a cold winter evening when you are curled up warm and cosy at home. I buy frozen Chinese spring roll pastry for this recipe and defrost it in the fridge overnight, then allow it to come to room temperature for a couple of hours before I use it. If you can't find spring roll pastry, you can use filo pastry instead, although obviously the texture will be much flakier.

SERVES 4–5 (MAKES 20)

¼ small green cabbage, grated into
  long shreds
1 medium carrot
1 small red pepper, deseeded
1 small green pepper, deseeded
100ml sunflower oil, plus more
  for frying
1 teaspoon cumin seeds
1 x 300g tin of sweetcorn, drained
1 teaspoon salt
150g red-skinned (unroasted, unsalted)
  peanuts, coarsely chopped or blended
100g tinned kidney beans
  (drained weight), rinsed
8 teaspoons plain flour
1 packet of Chinese spring roll
  or wonton pastry (at least 20 sheets)

Masala
4–6 fresh green chillies, seeds left in
3cm root ginger, peeled and
  roughly chopped
pinch of salt

Crush the chillies and ginger together with a pinch of salt using a pestle and mortar (or a blender), to make a fine masala paste.

Grate the cabbage and carrot into a large bowl. Grate the peppers and immediately add to the grated cabbage and carrot – grated pepper releases its juice very quickly, and if you lose the juice, you lose the flavour. Stir everything together.

Heat the oil and cumin seeds in a large pan over a medium heat. When the cumin seeds start to turn light brown, stir in the sweetcorn, masala paste, salt and peanuts. Cook for 3 minutes, stirring regularly. Remove from the heat, stir in the kidney beans and leave to cool for 15 minutes. Add the grated vegetables and toss the mixture with your hands to combine the filling ingredients thoroughly. Season to taste and set aside.

Put the flour into a small bowl, slowly add 100ml of cold water, and whisk to a smooth sticky paste for sealing the spring rolls.

Remove the pastry sheets from the packet and cover with a damp cloth to stop them drying out. Take one sheet of pastry and place it on a baking sheet or work surface with one of the short ends closest to you. Heap 3 teaspoons of the filling on to the pastry (about 2cm in from the edge nearest to you) and form into a sausage-shape across it, leaving a couple of centimetres uncovered along the closest edge and at the sides. Fold the pastry edge closest to you over the filling, then fold the sides of the pastry in towards the centre so that the filling is enclosed.

Roll up to form a tube of filled pastry until only about 2cm of unrolled pastry remains. Brush a little flour/water paste along the top edge of the pastry, then finish rolling. Place on a baking tray, seam side down. Repeat the process until you have 20 filled rolls.

Heat the frying oil – about 15cm deep – in a large pan over a high heat (or in a deep fat fryer, if you have one). Test the temperature by dropping a few little pieces of unused pastry into the oil – when it is hot enough, they will float to the surface. Reduce the heat to medium.

Gently lower 4 or 5 spring rolls into the oil and use a wooden spoon to move them around so that they cook evenly all over. Fry for about 6 minutes, or until golden brown and crispy. Remove from the oil with a slotted spoon and leave to rest on kitchen paper while you fry the next batch. Repeat until all the rolls have been fried.

Serve while still warm, with *lila dhania lasan* relish (page 203).

VARIATION – BAKED SPRING ROLLS

If you are looking for a healthier option to deep-frying, you can oven-bake your spring rolls. Preheat the oven to 180°C/160°C fan/gas mark 4 and oil a baking tray. Place the uncooked rolls on the tray, brush or spray with oil and cook for 30 minutes, turning after the first 10 minutes to help them crisp up evenly.

Bataka vada –
Lemon and coriander potato balls

(V, WF)

This is a simple starter that packs an amazing flavour. Bataka vada have been sold at Prashad ever since the first day the deli opened in 1992, and they remain immensely popular. The citrussy coriander leaves and the lemon juice go together beautifully and balance the starchy potatoes and the sweetness of the sultanas and coconut. It is important to boil the potatoes in their skins and then peel them after cooking, so that they don't absorb too much water.

SERVES 4 (MAKES 16)

sunflower oil, for oiling your
   hands and for frying

Masala
2–3 fresh green chillies, seeds left in
2–3 cloves of garlic
pinch of salt

Batter
150g chickpea flour
½ teaspoon salt
1 teaspoon medium red chilli powder

Filling
3 medium red-skinned
   (or other waxy) potatoes
1 teaspoon salt
2 teaspoons sugar (optional)
2 handfuls of fresh coriander,
   finely chopped
pinch of turmeric
4 teaspoons sesame seeds
4 tablespoons fresh coconut,
   grated (or unsweetened
   desiccated coconut)
4 teaspoons lemon juice
15g sultanas

Crush the chillies and garlic together with a pinch of salt using a pestle and mortar (or a blender), to make a fine masala paste.

Put the batter ingredients into a medium bowl, add 225ml of cold water, and stir until the mixture comes together – it should be thickly runny, with a similar texture to treacle.

Boil the potatoes in their skins for 40 minutes or so, until a knife tip will slide in easily, then peel and mash. Put the mashed potato into a large bowl with the masala paste and the rest of the filling ingredients and combine, taking care not to overwork the potatoes. Lightly oil your hands and roll this dryish mixture into 16 balls, each about 3cm in diameter.

Heat the frying oil – about 20cm deep – in a large pan over a high heat (or in a deep fat fryer, if you have one). Test the temperature by sprinkling a few drops of batter into the oil – when it is hot enough, they will float to the surface. Reduce the heat to medium.

Drop 5 potato balls into the batter mixture and carefully roll them around to make sure they are fully coated. Gently lower them into the oil and fry for about 3 minutes, moving them around with a wooden spoon to stop them sticking to the pan. When the batter is crisp and golden brown, remove them from the oil and leave them to rest on kitchen paper while you batter and fry the remaining *bataka vada* in batches.

Serve while still warm, with *kacha* tomato (page 207) or *lila dhania lasan* relish (page 203).

Dhal vada ~
Fluffy chickpea and chilli dough balls
(V, WF, OG, N)

This is quite a simple starter but very tasty – light fluffy dough balls with masses of flavour and a chilli kick. I make these for my mum when she visits from India, and she is always pleased to see me make perfectly uniform doughballs (don't worry if yours look a little wonky at first). You can buy magaj flour (coarsely ground gram flour) *and* chana dhal *in Indian supermarkets or online. Note that you will need to start soaking the* dhal *and flour at least 8 hours before you want to cook these.*

185g *chana dhal*
 (Bengal gram *dhal*/
 split skinned black chickpeas)
60g *magaj* flour
5cm root ginger, peeled and
 roughly chopped
2–6 fresh green chillies, seeds left in
1 teaspoon salt
2 handfuls of fresh coriander,
 finely chopped
sunflower oil, for frying

Rinse the *chana dhal* in warm water (see page 25), then drain. Place it in a medium bowl and cover with 1 litre of warm water. In a separate bowl mix the *magaj* flour with 50ml of warm water. Leave both to soak for at least 8 hours, or overnight.

Rinse the soaked *chana dhal* twice, then drain. Blend in a food processor with 2 tablespoons of cold water until it forms a medium coarse paste. Tip into a medium bowl and mix in the *magaj* flour, which will have slightly solidified after soaking, to form a batter.

Blitz the ginger in a blender (or use a pestle and mortar) to form a fine paste. Cut the chillies into 2mm-wide rings – keeping the ring shape is part of the beauty of this dish. Mix the ginger paste and chilli rings into the batter along with the salt, coriander and 75ml of cold water, stirring to get as much air into the mixture as possible. You can either use a long-handled ladle to stir the mixture or, if you have a beater attachment for your food processor, put the mixture on low speed for 1 minute, then medium for about 3 minutes, until the batter is light and full of air.

Heat the frying oil – about 15cm deep – in a large pan over a high heat (or in a deep fat fryer, if you have one). Test the temperature by sprinkling a few drops of batter into the oil – when it is hot enough, they will float to the surface.

Using the fingers of one hand, scoop a handful of batter up the side of the bowl. Keeping it in your fingers as opposed to your palm, hold it over the pan and gently push it off your hand and into the oil using your thumb – there's a trick to this but you'll quickly get it! (If you're feeling nervous, use one tablespoon to scoop up the mixture and another to push it into the oil – you won't end up with round *dhal vada* but the taste will be the same.) Repeat until the pan or fryer is half-filled with dough balls.

Check the underside of the *vada* after a minute or two, as they go brown quite quickly. Turn them over and cook the other side for a couple of minutes, then, once they're golden brown and crisp all over, remove them from the oil and leave them to rest on kitchen paper while you fry the next batch. Repeat until all the batter is used up.

Serve while still warm, with *kacha* tomato relish (page 207) or *safarjan wattana* (page 208).

Wattana ni kachori –
Spiced pea and garlic chapatti balls

(V)

Kachoris are a traditional Gujarati snack, often filled with spiced moong or tuvar dhal. I find that using green peas instead of pulses gives them a fresher, sweeter flavour that combines wonderfully with the warmth of the spices and the crunch of the peanuts. Adding citric acid to the dough and filling helps to keep the chapatti casing crisp and adds a little citrus zing to balance the flavours.

SERVES 4 (MAKES 20)

sunflower oil, for frying

Masala
1–3 fresh green chillies, seeds left in
1–3 cloves of garlic
2cm root ginger, peeled and
  roughly chopped
pinch of salt

Filling
200g frozen peas
50ml sunflower oil
¼ teaspoon brown mustard seeds
¼ teaspoon asafetida
pinch of turmeric
50g red-skinned (unroasted,
  unsalted) peanuts, coarsely chopped
  or blended
1 teaspoon salt
pinch of sugar
½ teaspoon medium red chilli powder
1 handful of fresh coriander,
  finely chopped
¼ teaspoon citric acid or
  1 teaspoon lemon juice
½ teaspoon *garam masala*

Crush the chillies, garlic and ginger together with a pinch of salt using a pestle and mortar (or a blender), to make a fine masala paste.

Rinse the peas in warm water to start them thawing, then chop them coarsely with a sharp knife or in a blender. Heat the oil and mustard seeds in a small/medium pan over medium heat. When the seeds start to pop, stir in the masala paste, chopped peas, asafetida, turmeric, peanuts, salt, sugar, chilli powder and half the coriander. Reduce the heat to low, cover the pan and leave to cook for 5 minutes. Remove from the heat and stir in the remaining coriander, the citric acid and the *garam masala*. Spread the filling out on a large flat tray or baking dish and allow to cool. Once cooled, use your hands to form the filling into 20 tightly rolled balls, each about 2cm in diameter.

Put the flour, salt and citric acid into a medium bowl and stir in the oil and 200ml of boiling water. Once the mixture starts to come together, use your hands to work it into a smooth dough. Divide the dough into 20 pieces and form each piece into a ball. Place on a lightly floured work surface and flatten the balls into discs measuring about 7cm in diameter and about 5mm thick. Cover with a damp tea towel to stop them drying out. Place a dough disc on the palm of your hand and put a ball of filling in the middle. Gently fold the casing

Dough

300g plain flour
½ teaspoon salt
½ teaspoon citric acid
8 teaspoons sunflower oil

upwards to form a parcel around the filling. Remove any excess dough where the edges meet at the top, and nip together any cracks that may have appeared. Gently roll the *kachori* between your palms to round it off, then place on a lightly oiled baking tray. Repeat with the remaining dough and filling balls.

Heat the frying oil – about 20cm deep – in a large pan over a high heat (or in a deep fat fryer, if you have one). Test the temperature by dropping a few pieces of leftover dough into the oil – when it is hot enough, they will float to the surface. Reduce the heat to medium. If you fry them at a very high heat, they will brown quickly but they won't be fully crisped up and will tend to go soggy once they cool.

Gently lower 4 or 5 *kachori* into the oil and use a wooden spoon to move them around so that they cook evenly all over. Fry for about 5 minutes or until golden brown and crispy. Remove from the oil with a slotted spoon and leave to rest on kitchen paper while you fry the next batch. Repeat until all the *kachori* have been fried.

Serve while still warm, with *kacha* tomato relish (page 207) or *shimla mirch* relish (page 206).

VARIATION – BAKED KACHORI

If you are looking for a healthier option to deep-frying, you can oven-bake your *kachori*. Preheat the oven to 180°C/160°C fan/gas mark 4 and oil a baking tray. Place the uncooked *kachori* on the tray, brush or spray with oil and cook for 40 minutes, turning after the first 10 minutes to help them crisp up evenly

Pethis –
Garlic-coconut filled potato balls

(V, N)

These are incredibly tasty, with their crisp golden coating and rich garlicky coconut centre. In Navsari (a city in the Surat region of India) there is a deli that is famous for its 'mama ni pethis'. My daughter Hina went there while travelling through India and was able to learn how to make them. On her return, she explained it to me, I modified the recipe and added my own signature touches . . . and Prashad's famous pethis *were born. Twenty-two years on, my recipe hasn't changed and* pethis *remain a firm favourite at the restaurant. Now I'm sharing my secret recipe with you – enjoy!*

SERVES 4–5 (MAKES 16–20)

sunflower oil, for frying

Masala

4–8 fresh green chillies, seeds left in
3–6 cloves of garlic
2cm root ginger, peeled and
  roughly chopped
pinch of salt

Filling

150g fresh coconut, grated
3 handfuls of fresh coriander,
  blended to a medium coarse paste
1½ teaspoons salt
5 teaspoons sugar
pinch of turmeric
75g *sev* (Indian chickpea vermicelli),
  blended to a coarse texture
5 teaspoons lemon juice
50g sultanas

Coating

3 medium white potatoes
50g chickpea flour
25g plain flour
25g cornflour
½ teaspoon salt

Crush the chillies, garlic and ginger together with a pinch of salt using a pestle and mortar (or a blender), to make a fine masala paste.

Put all the filling ingredients into a medium bowl, add the masala paste and mix firmly to work all the flavours into the coconut. Use a teaspoon or your hands to form the filling into small balls roughly 2cm in diameter, placing them on a baking sheet as you go.

Boil the potatoes in their skins for 40 minutes or so, until a knife tip will slide in easily, then peel and mash. Put the mashed potato into a large bowl with the other coating ingredients and mix well. The mixture will be very sticky and may be difficult to work with bare hands, so my tip is to wear lightly oiled rubber gloves to stop things getting too messy! Scoop up 4 teaspoons of the potato mix, roll gently between your hands to form a ball, then pat down to flatten – the mixture should cover the palm of your hand and be about 5mm thick.

Place a coconut ball in the centre of the flattened potato and gently fold up the edges to enclose it. It is essential that there should be no cracks in the casing (otherwise oil will seep in during frying and the *pethis* will burst), so nip together any that appear, then roll the *pethi* into a smooth ball between your palms. Repeat until all the filling balls have been wrapped in potato.

Heat the frying oil – about 15cm deep – in a large pan over a high heat (or in a deep fat fryer, if you have one). Test the temperature by sprinkling a few pieces of leftover potato coating into the oil – when it is hot enough, they will float to the surface. Reduce the heat to medium.

Gently place 4 or 5 *pethis* in the oil and use a wooden spoon to move them around so that they cook evenly all over. Fry until golden brown and crisp – roughly 5 minutes. Remove from the oil with a slotted spoon and leave to rest on kitchen paper while you fry the next batch. Repeat until all the *pethis* have been fried.

Serve warm, with *safarjan wattana* chutney (page 208) or *shimla mirch* relish (page 207).

VARIATION – BAKED PETHIS

If you are looking for a healthier option to deep-frying, you can oven-bake your *pethis*. Preheat the oven to 180°C/160°C fan/gas mark 4 and oil a baking tray. Place the uncooked *pethis* on the tray, brush or spray with oil and cook for 30 minutes, turning after the first 10 minutes to crisp them evenly.

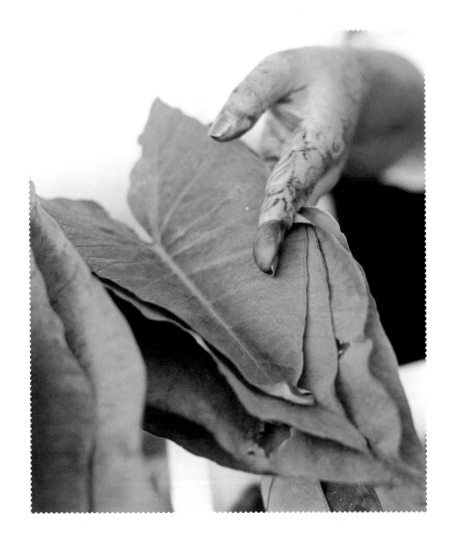

Bheta patra –
Shallow-fried colocasia leaf parcels

(HO)

This will always remind me of the semi-final of Gordon Ramsay's Best Restaurant competition – my goodness, what a challenging day! Gordon really liked the spiciness and soft delicate texture of this dish. The heart-shaped patra *leaves are sold in Indian supermarkets in small bundles. For this recipe I use small sweet leaves, about 10 x 15cm.*

16 small *patra* (colocasia) leaves

Masala

1–2 fresh green chillies, seeds left in
1–2 cloves of garlic
2cm root ginger, peeled and
  roughly chopped
pinch of salt

Paste

25g dried tamarind (from a block)
100g chickpea flour
1 tablespoon chapatti flour
2 teaspoons rice flour
1 teaspoon sugar
1 teaspoon salt
25g jaggery, finely chopped
  (or demerara/soft brown sugar)
1 teaspoon carom seeds
pinch of turmeric
1 tablespoon ground coriander
1 teaspoon *garam masala*
1 teaspoon sesame seeds
1 teaspoon plain live set yoghurt
8 teaspoons sunflower oil,
  plus 75ml for frying

Wash the *patra* leaves, then place them vein side up on a chopping board and slice off the thick central vein with a small sharp knife.

Crush the chillies, garlic and ginger together with a pinch of salt using a pestle and mortar (or a blender), to make a fine masala paste.

Soak the dried tamarind in 75ml of boiling water for 5 minutes, then pulp with your fingers. Sieve into a small bowl, squeezing the pulp to extract all the flavour.

Sieve the flours into a medium bowl. Add the masala paste, sugar, salt, jaggery, carom seeds, spices, sesame seeds, yoghurt and oil and mix well. Pour in the tamarind water and 100ml of warm water, mix to form a sticky but workable paste, then leave to rest for 10 minutes.

Pour 75ml of sunflower oil into a sturdy frying pan. Place one leaf vein side up on a chopping board or work surface, leaf tip furthest from you. Gently spread with about 3 teaspoons of paste to form a 5mm layer, taking care not to tear the leaf. Carefully lift the sides of the leaf and fold over to meet in the centre, then spread a layer of paste over the folded sections. Lift the nearest end of the leaf and fold it about 2cm on to itself, then continue to fold away from you until you reach the tip. Place the rolled leaf seam side down in the oiled pan. Repeat this process until all 16 leaves are pasted, folded and sitting in the pan.

Place the pan over a low heat, then cover and leave the *patra* parcels to cook for 10 minutes. Carefully turn them, then cover again and cook for a further 10 minutes. Turn them for a final time and cook covered for 8 minutes or so, until a sharp knife inserted in the middle comes out cleanly. The parcels will look dark in some places (where the leaf has hardened) and green in others – these variations give a fantastic texture.

Serve while still warm, with *shimla mirch* relish (page 206).

Bafela patra –
Stuffed colocasia leaf rolls

(V, HO)

Making these patra *rolls always takes me back to a busy Saturday morning twenty-two years ago, when I first opened my deli. I had made a batch of* bafela patra *to sell, and when my first customer of the day came in, I offered him a piece to try. He loved it so much that he bought the whole batch, so no one else got any that day! Colocasia leaves (see previous recipe) are also known as* taro, cocoyam *or* elephant-ear leaves. *I use medium leaves, about 20 x 20cm, for this recipe. I create my own steamer to cook the* patra, *but you can use a conventional steamer if you have one the right size.*

SERVES 4

8 medium *patra* (colocasia) leaves

Masala
2–4 fresh green chillies, seeds left in
2–4 cloves of garlic
3cm root ginger, peeled and
  roughly chopped
pinch of salt

Paste
50g dried tamarind (from a block)
200g chickpea flour
50g chapatti flour
50g rice flour
1½ teaspoons salt
40g jaggery, finely chopped
  (or demerara/soft brown sugar)
1½ teaspoons carom seeds
1 teaspoon turmeric
2–4 teaspoons ground coriander
1 tablespoon *garam masala*
1 teaspoon sesame seeds,
  plus 4 teaspoons to garnish
60ml sunflower oil

Wash the *patra* leaves, place them vein side up on a chopping board and slice off the thick central vein with a small sharp knife.

Crush the chillies, garlic and ginger together with a pinch of salt using a pestle and mortar (or a blender), to make a fine masala paste.

Soak the dried tamarind in 150ml of boiling water for 5 minutes, then pulp with your fingers and sieve into a small bowl, squeezing the pulp to get all the flavour out.

Sieve the flours together. Add the masala paste, salt, jaggery, carom seeds, spices, 1 teaspoon of sesame seeds and the oil and mix together well. Pour in the tamarind water and 200ml of warm water, mix to form a sticky but workable paste, then leave to rest for 10 minutes.

Put one of the larger leaves vein side up on a chopping board or work surface, leaf tip furthest from you. Gently spread with enough paste to cover with a 5mm layer (2 tablespoons should be sufficient), taking care not to tear the leaf. Now take a second leaf and lay it on top of the first, again vein side uppermost. Spread the surface of the new leaf with paste. Carefully lift the sides of the leaf stack and fold about 4cm in towards the centre, to give the stack straight sides. Spread a layer of paste over the leaf sections you have just folded in (the new top surface). Then gently lift the closest end of the *patra* leaf and fold it about 4cm on to itself, then fold again and continue to fold away from you until you reach the tip.

Repeat the pasting, layering, folding and rolling process 3 more times to use up the remaining 6 leaves, until you have 4 *patra* rolls.

Create a steamer by putting a flat-based heatproof bowl inside a large, deep pan. Pour water into the pan until it reaches most of the way up the bowl, leaving about 2cm of the rim sticking above the water, then place the pan over a high heat.

Lightly oil a plate with a 2cm rim that will fit into the pan. Put the 4 rolls seam side down on the plate and gently place it on top of the bowl. Put a lid on the pan, wrap a tea towel round the edge of the lid, and put a weight on top. Reduce the heat to medium and leave to steam for 35 minutes, turning the rolls after 15 minutes. Check that they are cooked by inserting a sharp knife into the middle of one – it should come out cleanly.

Carefully remove the plate from the steamer and leave to cool for 5 minutes. Put the *patra* on a chopping board and use a sharp knife to cut each one into 4 even slices. Drizzle with a little sunflower oil and sprinkle with sesame seeds.

Serve while still warm, with *kopru* dip (page 214) and a cup of hot *adhu vari chai* (page 228).

Handvo –
Seed-topped lentil cake

(WF, HO)

I make this savoury cake with my own handvo *flour, but if you are short of time, use 250g of ready-made* handvo *flour (ground mixed lentils and rice), which you can buy online and in Indian supermarkets. If you can't get hold of bottle gourd, use a quarter of a cabbage instead.*

SERVES 4

1 small or ½ medium bottle gourd,
  peeled and grated
1 small carrot, grated
1½ teaspoons salt
2 teaspoons sugar
8 teaspoons sunflower oil
1–2 dried red chillies
1 teaspoon cumin seeds
1 teaspoon brown mustard seeds
2 cloves
5 pieces of cinnamon
  (each about 1cm long)
4 teaspoons sesame seeds
10 fresh curry leaves

Dough ferment
150g basmati rice
50g *tuvar dhal* (dried pigeon peas/
  yellow lentils)
25g *chana dhal* (Bengal gram *dhal*/
  split skinned black chickpeas)
25g *urad dhal* (white lentils)
100ml sunflower oil
1 teaspoon fenugreek seeds
pinch of turmeric
160g plain live set yoghurt

Masala
3–6 fresh green chillies, seeds left in
1–2 cloves of garlic
3cm root ginger, peeled and
  roughly chopped
pinch of salt

Grind the rice and dhals together in a blender until coarsely ground – don't make it too fine. Tip into a bowl, gently stir in the oil, fenugreek seeds, turmeric and 150ml of warm water, then add the yoghurt and mix thoroughly but with a light hand. Place the dough in an airtight container and leave to ferment for 12 hours in a warm place, until it has risen and has a slightly sour smell.

Once the dough has fermented, crush the chillies, garlic and ginger together with a pinch of salt using a pestle and mortar (or a blender), to make a fine masala paste.

Add the masala paste, grated bottle gourd and carrot, salt and sugar to the fermented dough and mix thoroughly but gently. Taste and adjust the seasoning as required, then leave to rest for 2–3 minutes. Lightly oil a non-stick baking tray. Pour the dough on to the tray and gently shake to make sure it covers the whole tray.

Preheat the oven to 250°C/230°C fan/gas mark 9. Put the oil into a small pan over a medium heat for 1 minute before tipping in the red chilli(es), cumin seeds and mustard seeds. Once the mustard seeds start to pop, add the cloves and cinnamon and take the pan off the heat. Add the sesame seeds and curry leaves, but be careful, as the moisture in the leaves will make the oil sizzle. Use a tablespoon to pour the hot oil mixture over the dough, making sure it is thoroughly coated.

Place the tray on the middle shelf of the oven and bake for 75–80 minutes, or until the top is dark golden brown. Leave to cool in the tray for 10 minutes before cutting. Serve while still warm, with *shimla mirch* relish (page 206).

Dhokra –
Spicy chickpea cake

(WF, OG, N, HO)

Prashad's dhokra is one of the dishes of which I am most proud. My husband Mohan helped me to perfect the recipe, which has been used every day for the last twenty-two years to make the best dhokra I've ever tasted. Right from the start it was our fastest-selling and most popular starter in the deli – people would queue outside the door every Saturday morning to buy it. I make the dough the evening before so that it can ferment overnight, and I also create my own steamer to cook the dhokra, but you can use a conventional steamer if you have one big enough. My grandmother taught me this recipe using fruit salts as the raising agent, but if you don't have any, use baking powder instead.

SERVES 8

20g sugar
1 teaspoon salt
1 teaspoon fruit salts
　(or baking powder)

Dough ferment
175g chickpea flour
25g coarse semolina
115g plain live set yoghurt
pinch of turmeric
60ml sunflower oil

Masala
1–2 fresh green chillies, seeds left in
1–2cm root ginger, peeled and
　roughly chopped
pinch of salt

To finish
100ml sunflower oil
4 teaspoons brown mustard seeds
1 handful of fresh coriander,
　finely chopped

Blitz the flour, semolina, yoghurt, turmeric, oil and 200ml of warm water together using a hand-held blender or a food processor until the mixture is smooth. If you don't have a blender, you can mix this by hand using a slotted spoon – it will obviously take more time and a lot more effort, but it'll be a great bicep workout! Place the dough in an airtight container and leave to ferment for 12 hours in a warm place until it has risen and has a slightly sour smell.

Once the dough has fermented, crush the chillies and ginger together with a pinch of salt using a pestle and mortar (or a blender), to make a fine masala paste. Add the masala paste, sugar, salt and 2 tablespoons of warm water to the fermented dough and mix well.

Create a steamer by putting a flat-based heatproof bowl inside a large, deep pan. Pour water into the pan until it reaches most of the way up the bowl, leaving about 2cm of the rim sticking above the water, then place the pan over a high heat.

Lightly oil a plate with a 4cm rim that will fit into the pan. Once the water in the steamer is boiling, place the oiled plate on top of the bowl. Quickly mix the fruit salts into the dough and pour it on to the plate, making sure it goes right up to the edges of the rim. Put a lid on the pan, wrap a tea towel round the edge of the lid, and put a weight on top. Reduce the heat to medium, then leave to cook for 30 minutes.

While the *dhokra* is cooking, put the sunflower oil into a small pan over a medium heat. Tip in the mustard seeds and continue to heat until they start to pop. Remove the pan from the heat and carefully pour in 2 tablespoons of warm water. Place the pan back on the heat, bring to the boil and simmer until the mixture has reduced by half.

After the *dhokra* has had 30 minutes' cooking, check whether it is done by inserting a sharp knife into the middle – it should come out cleanly. Carefully remove the plate from the steamer and leave to cool for 15 minutes.

Cut into roughly 2cm squares while still on the plate, then use a spatula to lift them on to a serving plate. Drizzle sparingly with the mustard seed topping, sprinkle with the fresh coriander, and serve while still warm, with *rai marcha* (page 198) and *safarjan wattana* (page 208).

Kakdi na panella –
Garlicky cucumber and rice cake

(V, WF, N, HO)

*This is a lovely, healthy steamed dish that always reminds me of monsoon season in India –
I used to run out in the rain into my grandma's garden to pick the baby cucumbers, which hung so
low from the vine they nearly touched the ground. I create my own steamer to cook the* kakdi na
panella, *but you can use a conventional steamer if you have one the right size. Rice flour is not only
tasty but is also a great substitute for wheat flour if you want to avoid gluten in your cooking.*

SERVES 4

Masala

4–6 fresh green chillies,
  seeds left in
4–6 cloves of garlic
4cm root ginger, peeled and
  roughly chopped
pinch of salt

Dough

2 medium cucumbers
  (about 30cm long)
250g rice flour
100g cornflour
2 teaspoons salt
pinch of turmeric
1½ teaspoons sugar (optional)
1 handful of fresh coriander,
  coarsely chopped

To finish

50ml sunflower oil
1 handful of fresh coriander,
  finely chopped

Crush the chillies, garlic and ginger together with a
pinch of salt using a pestle and mortar (or a blender),
to make a fine masala paste.

Grate the cucumbers with a handheld grater or food
processor grater attachment. Put the grated cucumbers
and their juice into a large bowl with the masala paste,
rice flour, cornflour, salt, turmeric, sugar (if using),
coriander and 50ml of warm water. Mix well to form
a thick viscous dough (too liquid to lift from the bowl
but not fluid enough to pour). Season with additional
salt to taste.

Create a steamer by putting a flat-based heatproof
bowl inside a large, deep pan. Pour water into the pan
until it reaches most of the way up the bowl, leaving
about 2cm of the rim sticking above the water. Place
the pan over a high heat.

Lightly oil a plate with a 2cm rim that will fit into the
pan. Tip the dough on to the oiled plate and carefully
place it on top of the bowl. Put the lid on the pan, wrap
a tea towel round the edge of the lid, and put a weight
on top. Reduce the heat to medium, then leave to steam
for 30 minutes.

Check to see whether it is done by inserting a sharp knife into the middle – it should come out
cleanly. Carefully remove the plate from the steamer and leave to cool for 5 minutes. Cut the
kakdi na panella in quarters, then use a spatula to lift them on to small plates.

Drizzle with sunflower oil, sprinkle with chopped coriander and serve while still warm, with plenty
of *lila dhania lasan* (page 203) and a cup of steaming *adhu vari chai* (page 228).

Hara bara kebab –
Mashed pea and cauliflower kebabs

(V, N)

It's always refreshing when you get to taste something new. My daughter-in-law Minal first introduced these amazing vegetable kebabs to our restaurant menu in 2004, and I was really impressed. My son Bobby is a very lucky man!

SERVES 4 (MAKES 12)

80g fresh or frozen peas
1 small red-skinned (or other waxy) potato
¼ head of cauliflower, coarsely grated
¼ head of cabbage, coarsely grated
½ medium carrot, coarsely grated
1 handful of fresh coriander, finely chopped
30g chapatti flour
30g rice flour
½ teaspoon *garam masala*
1 teaspoon salt
½ teaspoon black peppercorns, coarsely ground or crushed
1 tablespoon lemon juice
sunflower oil, for oiling and frying

Masala

1–3 fresh green chillies, seeds left in
1–2 cloves of garlic
2cm root ginger, peeled and roughly chopped
pinch of salt

Crush the chillies, garlic and ginger together with a pinch of salt using a pestle and mortar (or a blender), to make a fine masala paste.

If you are using frozen peas, rinse them in warm water to start them thawing. Chop the peas with a sharp knife or in a blender until coarsely blended. Boil the potato in its skin, then peel and grate coarsely.

Put the masala paste, peas, grated potato and all the other ingredients except the sunflower oil into a large bowl. Mix thoroughly until you have a strong but workable dough-like paste. Lightly oil your hands and, taking 3 teaspoons at a time, form the mixture into flattened round patties. Place on an oiled tray.

Heat the frying oil – about 15cm deep – in a large pan over a high heat (or in a deep fat fryer, if you have one). Test the temperature by dropping a little of the kebab mix into the oil – when it is hot enough, the mix will float to the surface. Reduce the heat to medium.

Gently lower 4 or 5 kebabs into the oil and use a wooden spoon to move them around so that they cook evenly all over. Fry for 8–9 minutes, or until dark brown with a crisp coating. Remove from the oil with a slotted spoon and leave to rest on kitchen paper while you fry the next batch. Repeat until all the kebabs have been fried.

Serve while still warm, with *shimla mirch* relish (page 206).

Ratalu puri –
Spicy peanut-marinated purple yam and potato

(V, WF, OG, HO)

As far as I am concerned, this is the perfect steamed starter, healthy and full of flavour. Admittedly I love any purple yam dish, but this is my favourite – the bright violet-coloured yam is delicious (and decorative), and the combination of potatoes and purple yam is a delight. The addition of sugar is traditional and I think the dish tastes better with it, but you can omit it if you prefer. I create my own steamer to cook this, but you can use a conventional steamer if you have one big enough.

50g red-skinned (unsalted, unroasted)
  peanuts, coarsely chopped or blended
½ fresh coconut, grated (about 50g)
2 handfuls of fresh coriander,
  finely chopped
1½ teaspoons salt
4 teaspoons sugar (optional)
pinch of turmeric
4 tablespoons sesame seeds
100ml sunflower oil
1 large red-skinned (or other waxy)
  potato, peeled, halved and
  cut into 5mm slices
1 medium purple yam, peeled,
  halved and cut into 5mm slices
1 lemon, quartered, to serve

Masala

4–6 fresh green chillies, seeds left in
2cm root ginger, peeled and
  roughly chopped
pinch of salt

Crush the chillies and ginger together with a pinch of salt using a pestle and mortar (or a blender), to make a fine masala paste.

Put the masala paste, peanuts, coconut, coriander, salt, sugar (if using), turmeric, sesame seeds and oil into a medium bowl and mix, preferably with your hands. Don't leave this to stand for too long, otherwise the vegetables will release their juices and make it watery.

Create a steamer by putting a flat-based heatproof bowl inside a large, deep pan. Pour water into the pan until it reaches most of the way up the bowl, leaving about 2cm of the rim sticking above the water, then place the pan over a high heat.

Lightly oil a plate with a 2cm rim that will fit into the pan. Cover half the plate with potato slices and the other half with yam slices, then spoon the marinade over them to create a generous layer. Cover with the remaining slices of potato and yam, following the same pattern of potato on one half of the plate and yam on the other. (You can build up more layers of yam and potato if you prefer – just make sure you leave enough marinade to sandwich between each layer.)

Carefully place the plate on top of the bowl. Put the lid on the pan, wrap a tea towel round the edge of the lid, and put a weight on top. Reduce the heat to medium, then leave to cook for 25 minutes or so, until the vegetables are nice and tender.

Carefully remove the plate from the steamer. Spoon helpings into shallow bowls or dishes, making sure each one gets a good amount of marinade and a mixture of potato and purple yam. Serve piping hot, with the quartered lemon to squeeze over for a little fresh citrus zing.

Paneer tikka –
Griddled spicy paneer skewers
(WF, N, HO)

*Oh, this dish is so aromatic! I once cooked it on a family picnic at Bolton Abbey –
I remember other families nearby coming over to our barbecue, drawn by the wonderful scent
and very excited at what we were cooking. The unsalted fresh white cheese is fantastic with
strong flavoursome sauces, and the yoghurt in the marinade starts to break down the paneer and
the vegetables, allowing them to absorb even more flavour. I leave everything to infuse and
marinate overnight – if you want to prepare and cook this on the same day, just make sure you
allow at least 8 hours' marinating time. You will need 6 skewers, either metal or wooden,
but remember to soak wooden ones in water before cooking so that they don't burn.*

MAKES 6 SKEWERS

2 x 250g blocks of *paneer* cheese
1 medium red pepper,
  deseeded and cut into 6 pieces
1 medium green pepper,
  deseeded and cut into 6 pieces
1 medium Spanish onion,
  cut into 6 pieces
2 lemons, quartered, to serve

Marinade
2–3 fresh green chillies, seeds left in
4–8 cloves of garlic
2 handfuls of fresh coriander,
  finely chopped
2 teaspoons ground coriander
2 teaspoons *garam masala*
1½ teaspoons salt
1 teaspoon turmeric
2 tablespoons plain live set yoghurt
100ml sunflower oil

Blitz the chillies and garlic in a blender (or chop with
a sharp knife) until finely minced. Tip into a large bowl,
add the other marinade ingredients and mix well.

Cut each block of *paneer* into 9 equal-sized cubes
and add to the marinade along with the chopped
peppers and onion pieces. Stir to coat everything evenly,
then cover and leave in the refrigerator for at least
8 hours, or overnight.

Heat a lightly oiled griddle pan or fire up the barbecue
until good and hot. Thread each of your skewers with
3 pieces of *paneer*, 1 piece of onion and 1 piece of
each colour of pepper, alternating between *paneer* and
vegetables. Place on the griddle or barbecue and cook
for 20 minutes, until slightly charred, turning them
every 4–5 minutes to ensure they are cooked evenly on
each side.

Serve with the quartered lemons to squeeze over the
skewers, and with *kakadhi raitu* (page 212) and a fresh
green salad.

Pathudi –
Seed-topped chickpea pancake rolls

(WF, HO)

This is a delicate, delicious and intricate dish – you may need to try your hand at rolling the pancakes a few times before you perfect it, but it's worth the effort. It is my younger son Mayur's favourite, so my daughter-in-law Minal tries to ensure that she makes it for him whenever he comes to visit. You will need a large flat kitchen work surface or some flat baking trays on which to cool, cut and roll the pancakes. Have these ready before you start cooking the batter, as once it is cooked you'll need to work quickly.

SERVES 5–6

Masala

4–6 fresh green chillies, seeds left in
2 cloves of garlic
2cm root ginger, peeled and
  roughly chopped

Batter

250g chickpea flour, sieved
100g plain live set yoghurt
2 teaspoons salt
pinch of turmeric

Topping

100ml sunflower oil
1 teaspoon brown mustard seeds
1 tablespoon sesame seeds
2 handfuls of fresh coriander,
  finely chopped
50g fresh coconut, grated
  (or unsweetened desiccated
  coconut)

Crush the chillies, garlic and ginger together with a pinch of salt using a pestle and mortar (or a blender), to make a fine masala paste.

Whisk the chickpea flour, yoghurt and 600ml of warm water together in a medium bowl to form a smooth runny batter. Pour into a large non-stick pan, stir in the masala paste, salt and turmeric, place over a medium heat and continue to stir, making sure it doesn't stick to the bottom, as otherwise it will burn. When the batter starts to thicken (after 4–5 minutes), reduce the heat to low, cover and leave to cook for 5 minutes. Stir gently, taking care in case the mixture spits and bubbles, then cover again and leave to cook for a further 3 minutes.

Remove the pan from the heat and ladle batter on to your work surface or baking trays. Use a palette knife to spread it in a thin even layer, roughly 2mm thick, until it is all used up – I find I usually need 4 baking trays, each 25 x 40cm.

The batter will start to set as it cools. Leave for 5 minutes, then slice it into 5cm-wide strips. Starting at one end of a strip, use the palette knife to gently lift and roll it up.

When it is fully rolled up, slide the pancake roll on to the palette knife and place on a serving plate. Repeat until all the pancake strips have been rolled and stacked on the plate.

Heat the oil and mustard seeds in a small pan over a medium heat. Remove from the heat when the mustard seeds start to pop, then stir in the sesame seeds. Spoon the warm seed oil over the *pathudi*, making sure each roll gets a generous coating.

Sprinkle with the coriander and coconut to serve. This dish doesn't need anything else – it's perfect just as it is.

STREET SNACKS
AND NASTO

STREET SNACKS AND *NASTO*

You find a huge variety of street snacks on nearly every street corner in India, sold from stationary pushcarts and makeshift stalls. Different cities have different specialities, and residents pride themselves on the variety of dishes offered in the local *chaat* houses or *dhabas*. Some vendors are so well known that they draw crowds, clamouring to buy their food for lunch, for a quick snack, or just for the sheer pleasure of savouring the delights that are presented on paper plates or passed to outstretched hands from the tiny carts along the roadside.

The most famous street snack in northern India is *chaat*, a fabulous combination of deep-fried crunchy, creamy, spicy, sweet, tart flavours that will have you licking your lips and fingers and coming back for more (indeed, the name *chaat* comes from the Hindi verb *chaatna*, meaning to lick). This dish, the king of Indian streetfood, is a must-have at weddings and parties, where guests go mad for the tasty layers of *samosa* and *puri* pieces, chickpeas, potatoes, crunchy *sev*, chutney and yoghurt. Try my version and you'll see why …

Other traditional streetfood dishes include moreish *tikki puri* (fried dough puffs), *bataka* *pauwa* with its mixture of spicy potato, peanuts and flattened rice, and *bhel*, a form of *chaat* made with crispy puffed rice, potato, chickpeas, chapatti pieces, chutney, peanuts and a tangy blend of red onion and green mango, a dish which is so much more than its component parts – it has to be tasted to be believed!

Nasto is the Hindi word for snacks (one that is much used by Gujarati people, who are traditionally keen snackers), and covers everything from a little something to nibble at elevenses to light meals and fragrant breads to enjoy at any time of day. Filling dishes like *dhal dhokri* soup, garlicky *kamree* (savoury porridge) and *dai vada* (lentil dumplings) are great when you fancy something simple for supper, while *aloo gobi paratha* (stuffed flatbreads) and *thepla* (fenugreek chapatti) can be taken with you to eat on the go.

Snack meals are economical too – *vagarela* recipes are specifically designed to use up leftovers and turn them into delicious dishes in their own right … in fact, they are so tasty that I will often cook extra rice or bread the night before just so that I can make spiced-up *vagarela baath* or *rotli* the next day!

STREET SNACKS AND *NASTO*

Chaat –
The king of streetside India (chickpea, potato and samosa streetfood)

(N)

I am very proud of this dish – the sweet-sour-savoury, crunchy-creamy, simply delicious mixture of pastry, chickpeas, potatoes, sev, chutney and yoghurt is guaranteed to put a smile on anyone's face. My son Bobby is always amused by how crazy people go at weddings when this chaat *appears . . . chivalry and courtesy go out of the window as elegantly dressed guests sharpen their elbows and push through the queues to get their portion first! Get all the components of this dish ready before you assemble it, and serve it as soon as possible after putting it together.*

SERVES 4

1 large red-skinned
  (or other waxy) potato
100g chapatti flour, plus extra
  for flouring
2 teaspoons sunflower oil,
  plus extra for smoothing and frying
2 teaspoons lemon juice
¼ teaspoon salt
2 teaspoons cumin seeds
300g plain live set yoghurt
3½ teaspoons sugar
4 Gujarati mixed vegetable *samosas*
  (page 42)
1 x 400g tin of chickpeas, rinsed
  and drained
12 tablespoons *imli* chutney
  (page 210)
1 medium onion, finely diced
100g *sev* (Indian chickpea vermicelli)
4–8 teaspoons *lasan* chutney
  (page 209)
1 handful of fresh coriander,
  finely chopped

Boil the potato in its skin for 40 minutes or so, until a knife tip will slide in easily, then peel and cut into 1cm cubes.

Put the flour, oil, lemon juice and salt into a medium bowl with 40ml of warm water and use your hands to bring together and form a stiff dough. Knead for a minute or so, then smooth the surface with a little oil and leave to rest for 15 minutes.

Split the dough in two. Roll half of it out on a lightly floured work surface until about 2mm thick. Use a palette knife to cut into rectangles of roughly 2 x 1cm, placing them on a lightly oiled baking tray as you go. Repeat with the other half of the dough.

Heat the frying oil – about 10cm deep – in a large pan over a high heat (or in a deep fat fryer, if you have one). Test the temperature by dropping a few dough pieces into the oil – when it is hot enough, they will float to the surface. Reduce the heat to medium.

Using a slotted spoon, transfer 2 spoonfuls of dough pieces into the oil and use a wooden spoon to move them around so that they cook evenly. Fry for a minute or two until they start to turn golden brown. Remove from the oil with the slotted spoon and leave to rest on kitchen paper while you fry the next batch. Repeat until all the *puri* pieces have been fried.

Dry-roast the cumin seeds in a frying pan over a low heat for about a minute, until they start to darken slightly, shaking the pan to toast them evenly. Finely crush the roasted seeds using a pestle and mortar or a blender, then put them into a medium bowl with the yoghurt and sugar and whisk the mixture until runny.

Place 4 shallow dishes or bowls on the table or work surface. Break a *samosa* into small chunks and place in the bottom of each dish. Divide the fried *puri* pieces, potato cubes and chickpeas between the bowls, spreading them over the *samosas*. Drizzle each portion first with 3 tablespoons of *imli* chutney, then with 3 tablespoons of the yoghurt mixture. Sprinkle each one with a handful of the chopped onion, followed by a quarter of the *sev*. Finish with a drizzled teaspoon or two of *lasan* chutney and a sprinkling of coriander.

Serve immediately, explaining to your guests that *chaat* is a dish of many layers, so they should dig right down to the bottom to get a little bit of everything in each spoonful!

VARIATION – DRY-FRIED PURI

If you are looking for a healthier option to deep-frying, you can dry-fry the dough. Roll half of it out into a disc and place in a non-stick frying pan or on a *tawa* over a medium heat. Dry-fry for 2–3 minutes on each side until crisp, pressing down with a heatproof spatula while it cooks to remove any air. Remove from the pan and leave to rest on kitchen paper while you roll out and dry-fry the other half of the dough. Once cooled, break the discs into small pieces (roughly 2 x 1cm) to use in your *chaat*.

Kamree –
Savoury lentil porridge

(V, WF, N, HO)

Kamree is a combination of ground Bengal gram dhal *and* magaj *flour. You can buy* magaj *flour (coarsely ground gram flour) in Indian supermarkets or online. Note that you will need to start soaking the* dhal *and flour at least 6 hours before you want to cook this.*

SERVES 4

200g *chana dhal* (Bengal gram *dhal*/
  split skinned black chickpeas)
25g *magaj* flour
1½ teaspoons salt
¼ teaspoon turmeric
2 handfuls of fresh coriander,
  finely chopped
150ml sunflower oil
2–3 dried red chillies
2 teaspoons brown mustard seeds
¼ teaspoon asafetida
2 tablespoons sugar

Masala
2–4 fresh green chillies, seeds left in
5–6 cloves of garlic
6cm root ginger, peeled and
  roughly chopped
pinch of salt

To serve
80g *sev* (Indian chickpea vermicelli)
1 lemon, quartered

Rinse the *chana dhal* at least 3 times in hot water (see page 25), then put it into a large deep bowl and cover with about 1 litre of warm water. In a separate bowl mix the *magaj* flour with 60ml of warm water. Leave both to soak for at least 6 hours.

Crush the chillies, garlic and ginger with a pinch of salt using a pestle and mortar (or a blender), to make a fine masala paste.

Drain the *dhal* and grind in a food processor until medium-fine. Tip it into a medium bowl and add the *magaj* flour, which will have slightly solidified after soaking, along with the masala paste, salt, turmeric and half the chopped coriander. Mix well with your hands.

Put the oil and dried chillies into a large pan over a high heat for a minute or two, then stir in the mustard seeds. When they start to pop, stir in the asafetida and reduce the heat to low. Spoon in the spiced *dhal*/flour mixture and stir throughly. Cover and cook for 3 minutes, stirring occasionally to prevent sticking and scorching, then gradually pour in 650ml of boiling water and stir thoroughly but carefully, as the *dhal* may splash up. Increase the heat to high and bring to the boil, taking care not to stand over it, as it may bubble and spit.

Cover the pan again, then reduce the heat to low and simmer for 8–10 minutes, stirring occasionally.

Stir in the sugar and leave to cook for a further 5–6 minutes over a low heat, stirring every so often to loosen any *dhal* that sticks to the bottom of the pan (don't worry about this – it adds texture!).

Remove from the heat, sprinkle with the remaining chopped coriander and leave to rest, uncovered, for 15 minutes, stirring occasionally, while the flavours develop.

Serve warm, in wide, shallow bowls with a generous sprinkling of *sev* on top and lemon quarters for squeezing over. Any leftovers can be stored in an airtight container in the fridge for a couple of days (when reheating, add a splash of water, as this porridge-like *dhal* will solidify as it cools).

Dhal dhokri –
Indian pasta and pigeon pea soup

(V, N, HO)

This is a tasty one-dish meal, ideal for a cosy Sunday supper – or, in the case of my family, a cosy Monday supper, as that is our day off from the restaurant. Pigeon peas are a great source of protein, and the combination with chickpea pasta makes for a really satisfying dish. Perfect for cold dark evenings when all you want to do is curl up on the sofa in front of a Bollywood movie, with a bowl of fragrant, warming comfort food and a large spoon.

SERVES 4

Masala

2–3 fresh green chillies, seeds left in
2–3 cloves of garlic
pinch of salt

Ginger paste

4cm root ginger, peeled and
  roughly chopped
pinch of salt

Dhal soup

200g *tuvar dhal* (dried pigeon peas/
  yellow lentils)
1 teaspoon sunflower oil
1 x 400g tin of peeled plum
  tomatoes, blended
2 teaspoons salt
1½ teaspoons turmeric
1 teaspoon medium red chilli powder
40g jaggery, finely chopped
  (or demerara/soft brown sugar)
1 handful of fresh coriander,
  finely chopped

Tarka (spiced oil)

40ml sunflower oil
1 teaspoon cumin seeds
1 teaspoon brown mustard seeds
½ teaspoon asafetida
½ handful of fresh coriander,
  finely chopped

Crush the chillies and garlic with a pinch of salt using a pestle and mortar (or a blender), to make a fine masala paste. Separately crush the root ginger with a pinch of salt using a pestle and mortar (or a blender), to make a fine paste.

Rinse the *tuvar dhal* at least 3 times in hot water (see page 25), then put it into a very large pan with 1.8 litres of boiling water. Bring to the boil, then simmer over a medium heat for a couple of minutes until it starts to foam. Skim the froth from the surface, add the teaspoon of oil and simmer three-quarters covered for about 40 minutes, stirring occasionally, until the *dhal* is soft and cooked through.

Remove from the heat, add the tomatoes and 1.3 litres of warm water, and blitz with a hand-held blender or in a food processor until smooth. Return to a medium heat, stir in the remaining *dhal* soup ingredients and the ginger paste, then bring to the boil and leave to simmer for 8–10 minutes while you prepare the *tarka*.

Heat the oil in a small pan over a high heat for a minute, then add the cumin and mustard seeds. As soon as the mustard seeds start to pop, reduce the heat to low and stir in the asafetida and coriander (taking care, as the oil may spit). Tip the *tarka* into the *dhal* soup and stir through. Simmer the soup uncovered for about 20 minutes over a medium heat while you prepare the Indian pasta.

Indian pasta

100g chickpea flour, sieved,
  plus extra for flouring
100g chapatti flour, sieved
25ml sunflower oil
1 teaspoon salt
½ teaspoon turmeric
½ teaspoon cumin seeds
2 teaspoons sugar
1 handful of fresh coriander,
  finely chopped

To serve

1 medium carrot, finely diced
1 medium red onion, finely diced
sunflower oil, for drizzling
1 lemon, quartered

Put the flours, masala paste, oil, salt, turmeric, cumin seeds and sugar into a medium bowl and mix thoroughly. Add the chopped coriander, pour in 75ml of warm water and stir – it will be quite sticky. Knead the pasta dough for a couple of minutes, then divide in two. Form one half into a ball, place on a lightly floured work surface, sprinkle with a little chickpea flour and roll out until 5mm thick. Use a palette knife to cut the dough into bite-size pieces – I like to make little squares, about 3 x 3cm, but you can make whatever shapes you like. Place the pasta shapes in the soup as you cut them. Repeat with the other half of the dough.

Simmer the soup for a further 5 minutes or so over a low heat, stirring occasionally and seasoning to taste, then remove from the heat and set aside to rest, covered, for at least 5 minutes, to allow the flavours to develop.

Serve generous portions in large soup bowls, with a sprinkle of carrot and red onion and a drizzle of oil on top, and lemon quarters for squeezing over.

Dai vada ~
Lentil dumplings with cumin yoghurt

(WF, OG, N)

*This is a typical Gujarati dish: tangy, sweet, light and refreshing. Dai vada is
perfect as a light meal (or a starter) on a hot summer's day, with its cooling combination
of creamy yoghurt and chilled dumplings. Note that the lentils need to soak for 8 hours
before you start cooking this dish.*

100g *urad dhal* (white lentils)

100g *masoor dhal* (split red lentils)

4–6 fresh green chillies, seeds left in

4cm root ginger, peeled
  and roughly chopped

pinch of salt, plus ½ teaspoon
  for the batter

540g plain live set yoghurt

1½ teaspoons cumin seeds,
  roasted* and finely crushed

4 teaspoons sugar

sunflower oil, for frying

To serve

1 teaspoon medium red chilli powder

1 teaspoon cumin seeds,
  roasted* and finely crushed

12 tablespoons *imli* chutney (page 210)

1 handful of fresh coriander,
  finely chopped

* SEE TOP TIPS (PAGE 26)
FOR HOW TO ROAST
CUMIN SEEDS.

Rinse the *urad dhal* and *masoor dhal* 3 times in warm water (see page 25), then place in a bowl, cover with cold water and leave to soak for at least 8 hours.

Drain the soaked *dhal*, then blitz in a food processor until finely ground, stopping as necessary and using a spatula to push down any that try to escape up the sides. Tip into a medium bowl.

Crush the chillies and ginger together with a pinch of salt using a pestle and mortar (or a blender), to make a fine masala paste.

Add the masala and half a teaspoon of salt to the ground *dhal* and stir well to form a thick batter. Try to get as much air into the mixture as possible, as this will make a big difference to the texture of the *vada*. If you have a beater attachment for your food processor, put the mixture on low speed for 5 minutes, until the batter is light and full of air.

Put the yoghurt into a large bowl with 20ml of cold water and whisk until smooth and runny. Stir in the crushed cumin seeds and sugar, then set aside.

Heat the frying oil – about 20cm deep – in a large pan over a high heat (or in a deep fat fryer, if you have one) Test the temperature by sprinkling a few drops of batter into the oil – when it is hot enough, they will float to the surface. Reduce the heat to medium. Fill a large bowl with cold water and place it nearby.

Gently slide tablespoonfuls of batter into the hot oil until the pan or fryer is half-filled. Check the underside of the *vada* after a minute or two, as they go brown quite quickly. Turn them to cook the other side for a couple of minutes, then, once golden brown and crisp all over, remove from the oil and drop into the cold water while you fry the next batch. Repeat until all the dough is used up. You should aim to make at least 16 *vada*, as you will want at least 4 per person.

Spread 3 tablespoons of the cumin yoghurt in the bottom of each dish or bowl. Remove the *vada* from the water one at a time and gently squeeze between your palms to drain, taking care not to crack the dough. Put 4 *vada* into each bowl and top with 4 more tablespoons of yoghurt. Sprinkle a pinch or two of chilli and cumin seeds over the yoghurt, then drizzle 3 tablespoons of *imli* chutney over each serving, making sure you leave some of the yoghurt uncovered – part of the beauty of this dish is the colour contrast between the rich chutney and the pale yoghurt. Garnish with chopped coriander before serving.

Vagarela baath – Spiced-up rice

(WF, HO)

I have a long family connection with rice – my ancestors were rice farmers – and Gujarati cuisine involves rice in many different forms. This is a spicy snack version. My grandmother used to make this for me to take to school; her cooking was famous in our village, so my friends would always be interested to see (and taste) what she had packed for my lunch. Vagarela baath is traditionally made to use up leftover rice, but it tastes so good that it is worth cooking fresh rice (as in this recipe) in order to make it.

SERVES 4

250g basmati rice
1 tablespoon sunflower oil
1 teaspoon salt
½ teaspoon turmeric
1 medium onion, cut into 1cm cubes
1 handful of fresh coriander,
  finely chopped
½ teaspoon salt
50g red-skinned (unsalted, unroasted)
  peanuts, coarsely chopped
2 teaspoons sesame seeds
1 teaspoon sugar
100g plain live set yoghurt

Masala
2–4 fresh green chillies, seeds left in
2–3 cloves of garlic
pinch of salt

Tarka (spiced oil)
60ml sunflower oil
1 teaspoon cumin seeds
1 teaspoon brown mustard seeds

Crush the chillies and garlic together with a pinch of salt using a pestle and mortar (or a blender), to make a fine masala paste.

Rinse the rice 3 times under warm water, then drain. Stir the rice and oil together in a large pan over a high heat for 1 minute, then add the salt and 900ml of boiling water. Turn the heat up to high, cover and cook until the majority of the water has evaporated and there is only a little bubbling at the edges – this should take about 8–10 minutes.

Place a large piece of foil on top of the rice, tucking it in around the edges, then put the lid on. Reduce the heat to the lowest setting and leave to cook gently for 3 minutes, then remove from the heat and set aside for 1 minute to allow the rice to absorb any remaining water.

Spread the rice on a baking tray and leave it to cool for 4–5 minutes. Add the masala paste, turmeric, onion, coriander, salt, peanuts, sesame seeds, sugar and yoghurt, and mix in with your hands.

Heat the *tarka* oil for 30 seconds over a medium heat in the pan in which the rice was cooked. Stir in the cumin seeds and when they start to darken, add the mustard seeds. Once they start to pop, return the rice to the pan and stir. Reheat the rice over a medium heat for a minute or so, then turn the heat to low, cover and cook for a further minute.

Remove from the heat and leave to rest, uncovered, for a couple of minutes while the flavours develop. Serve in wide dishes or soup bowls, with *limbu attana* (page 196).

Vagareli rotli –
Chapatti in spicy yoghurt sauce
(N, HO)

Vagarela dishes are designed to use up leftovers from another meal, rather like bubble and squeak or refried beans. I make this dish from leftover rotlis *or* rotlas *cooked the night before – it's perfect for a speedy brunch, lunch or light supper.*

SERVES 4

10 *rotli* (page 170) or
  4 *juvar na rotla* (page 173)
100ml sunflower oil
1 teaspoon brown mustard seeds
1 teaspoon fenugreek seeds
1 teaspoon salt
½ teaspoon turmeric
1 tablespoon sugar
2 handfuls of fresh coriander,
  finely chopped
320g plain live set yoghurt

Masala

2–4 fresh green chillies, seeds left in
2–3 cloves of garlic
3cm root ginger, peeled and
  roughly chopped
pinch of salt

Crush the chillies, garlic and ginger together with a pinch of salt using a pestle and mortar (or a blender), to make a fine masala paste.

Break the *rotli/rotla* into roughly 2–3cm square pieces. Heat the oil in a large pan over a medium heat for 30 seconds, then add the mustard seeds. Once they start to pop, stir in the masala paste, *rotli/rotla* pieces, fenugreek seeds, salt, turmeric, sugar and half the coriander. Once the mixture starts sizzling, reduce the heat to low and cook for 2 minutes, stirring occasionally. Increase the heat to medium and cook for another 2 minutes, until the *rotli/rotla* pieces start to crisp up, stirring all the while to prevent anything from sticking.

Add the yoghurt and 100ml of warm water and stir well to combine. Increase the heat to high and keep stirring for about half a minute, until the mixture is piping hot again, then remove from the heat. Sprinkle with the remaining coriander and serve straight away, just as it is.

Vagareli makai –
Speedy spicy sweetcorn
(V, WF, HO)

I love visiting my daughter Hina in Chicago – I get to spend time with her, I get to play with my lovely grandson Tristan and (like every good mother-in-law) I get to spoil my son-in-law, Bhavesh. He loves this dish, so I make it fresh for him every morning. Vagareli makai is traditionally made with leftover corn-on-the-cob, but this quick and easy version uses tinned sweetcorn instead. You can use frozen if you prefer – just rinse it in warm water to start it thawing before cooking.

SERVES 4

75ml sunflower oil
1 teaspoon brown mustard seeds
¼ teaspoon asafetida
2 x 300g tins of sweetcorn, drained
pinch of turmeric
50g red-skinned (unsalted, unroasted)
  peanuts, coarsely chopped or blended
½ teaspoon salt
2 handfuls of fresh coriander,
  finely chopped
2 teaspoon sesame seeds
100g *sev* (Indian chickpea vermicelli),
  to serve
1 lemon, quartered, to serve

Masala
3–5 fresh green chillies, seeds left in
2–3 cloves of garlic
2cm root ginger, peeled and
  roughly chopped
pinch of salt

Crush the chillies, garlic and ginger together with a pinch of salt using a pestle and mortar (or a blender), to make a fine masala paste.

Heat the oil in a large pan over a high heat for 30 seconds, then add the mustard seeds. Once they start to pop, reduce the heat to low while you stir in the asafetida and sweetcorn, then return the heat to high again and fry together for a minute.

Add the masala paste and turmeric and stir for 30 seconds, then add the peanuts, salt, coriander and sesame seeds. Stir well, then reduce the heat to medium and leave to cook uncovered for 3 minutes, stirring occasionally. Remove from the heat and set aside to rest, covered, for at least 5 minutes while the flavours develop.

Serve with a sprinkling of *sev* over each helping, and with lemon quarters for squeezing over and a cup of steaming *adhu vari chai* (page 228).

Lasan mushroom –
Indian garlic mushrooms

(WF, N)

Occasionally when the family fancies a change from traditional Indian cuisine, we have an Italian-themed night. To start the meal, I always cook my take on garlic mushrooms – delicious, simple and packed full of flavour. Mushrooms work brilliantly in many types of dish, as they soak up spices and seasoning – here they are the perfect vehicle for garlicky chilli masala and citrussy coriander.

SERVES 4

2 tablespoons sunflower oil
2 teaspoons ground coriander
65g salted butter
1 teaspoon salt
500g button mushrooms, halved
2 handfuls of fresh coriander,
  finely chopped

Masala
5–6 fresh green chillies, seeds left in
5–6 cloves of garlic
pinch of salt

Salad
12 cherry tomatoes, halved
3 spring onions, finely chopped
1 tablespoon black peppercorns,
  coarsely ground or crushed

Crush the chillies and garlic together with a pinch of salt using a pestle and mortar (or a blender), to make a fine masala paste.

Heat the oil in a deep frying pan over a low heat for a minute, then stir in the masala paste and ground coriander. Leave to fry for a minute, then add the butter and salt. Once the butter has melted, tip in the mushrooms and fresh coriander. Increase the heat to full and stir to coat everything in the masala/butter mixture. Fry for 3–4 minutes, stirring all the time, until the moisture released by the mushrooms has evaporated.

Use your hands to mix the tomatoes, spring onions and crushed pepper together in a small bowl, then spoon this mixture on to one side of a serving dish or bowl. Tip the mushrooms on to the other side and let people serve themselves, getting a good mixture of fresh vegetables and fragrant buttery mushrooms in each helping.

Thepla –
Fragrant fenugreek chapatti

(N, HO)

If you have ever travelled with Gujarati people and watched them unwrap a foil package to enjoy a fragrant bread-type snack, the chances are that they were eating thepla. *Flavour-filled and easy to eat on the go,* thepla *is the perfect food for journeys and picnics.*

MAKES 12

sunflower oil, for frying

Masala

4–6 fresh green chillies, seeds left in
2–4 cloves of garlic
pinch of salt

Dough

410g chapatti flour
50g fresh fenugreek leaves,
 roughly chopped
½ teaspoon turmeric
1 teaspoon cumin seeds, roasted*
 and coarsely crushed
1 teaspoon cumin seeds (unroasted)
75ml sunflower oil
90g plain live set yoghurt
1½ teaspoons salt
2 teaspoons sugar

* SEE TOP TIPS (PAGE 26)
FOR HOW TO ROAST
CUMIN SEEDS.

Crush the chillies and garlic together with a pinch of salt using a pestle and mortar (or a blender), to make a fine masala paste.

Put the dough ingredients into a large bowl with 125ml of warm water and mix with your hands until the dough comes together. Knead it for 5 minutes, then divide into 12 roughly equal pieces. Roll them into balls between your palms and squash to flatten them slightly.

Place one of the flattened dough balls on a lightly floured work surface and roll it into a disc about 14cm in diameter and roughly 5mm thick, turning it as you roll and keeping the pressure light. Turn the dough 90° after every couple of rolls to keep it circular. (Don't worry too much about the shape: it is more important that the disc is of even thickness, and in time you will acquire the knack of making it perfectly round.) If you find the dough sticks to the work surface, sprinkle a little more flour underneath. Repeat with the remaining dough balls, placing the discs on a lightly oiled baking sheet as you go, making sure they don't overlap.

Put a flat *tawa* pan or a flat-based non-stick frying pan over a medium heat for a minute. Dry-fry a dough disc in the pan for about 90 seconds, flipping it over with a spatula every 10 seconds or so to cook both sides evenly.

Drizzle a teaspoon of oil around the edge of the pan. Use the spatula to press down and gently flatten the dough where it puffs up while cooking. Fry for about 30 seconds, then flip it over and cook the other side for a further 30 seconds. Remove from the pan and place on kitchen paper while you cook the remaining discs.

Enjoy hot, with a spoonful of plain yoghurt, some *limbu attana* pickle (page 196) and a cup of *adhu vari chai* (page 228). Alternatively, leave to cool before wrapping in foil to take on your next journey …

Methi bhaji pura –
Fenugreek and coriander pancakes

(N)

The aromas from this dish are amazing. I love the slightly bitter flavour of fenugreek leaves, but if you aren't a fan or find them hard to get hold of, or if you simply fancy trying something different, they can be replaced with grated cucumber, cauliflower, cabbage, spring onions, courgettes, carrots or pretty much any other firm vegetable that you fancy. The pan can get quite smoky, so make sure the kitchen windows are open and/or the extractor fan is on before you start.

SERVES 4 (MAKES ABOUT 12)

24 teaspoons sunflower oil, for frying

50ml ghee or clarified butter, melted, to serve

40g jaggery, grated (or demerara/ soft brown sugar), to serve

Masala

5–6 fresh green chillies, seeds left in

2–4 cloves of garlic

2cm root ginger, peeled and roughly chopped

pinch of salt

Batter

220g sorghum flour, sieved

60g chapatti flour, sieved

½ teaspoon turmeric

1½ teaspoons salt

1 teaspoon cumin seeds

150g plain live set yoghurt

2 teaspoons ground coriander

1 tablespoon sugar

100g fresh fenugreek leaves, roughly chopped

Crush the chillies, garlic and ginger together with a pinch of salt using a pestle and mortar (or a blender), to make a fine masala paste.

Mix the flours in a large bowl with your hands, running your fingers through to ensure that they are well combined. Add the masala paste and the remaining batter ingredients, pour in 375ml of warm water, and mix well to form a thick but runny batter. Season to taste.

Heat a couple of teaspoons of oil in a large frying pan over a medium heat for about 45 seconds and tilt to coat the whole pan. Use a small ladle to pour about 125ml of batter into the middle of the pan. Tilt the pan or use a palette knife to spread the batter to the edges. Reduce the heat to low, cover with a lid or foil and leave to cook for 1 minute.

Use a spatula to turn the pancake and fry uncovered for another 2 minutes or so. You can fry them for longer if you prefer – I tend to cook them slowly for a while until they are quite well done, almost black in parts, because my husband likes the charcoal taste, but you may prefer them less charred!

Make the rest of the pancakes the same way, dishing up as you go along or stacking them on a plate in a warm oven, until all the batter is used up. Serve with a drizzle of ghee or clarified butter and a small heap of jaggery flakes on the side, so you can scoop a little up every so often for the occasional sweeter mouthful in between spicy ones.

Aloo gobi paratha ~
Potato and cauliflower stuffed flatbread

(OG, N, HO)

I often make this for brunch on a Sunday for the family and restaurant staff, as a treat before our day off on Monday. I recommend that you use two frying pans to cook these (the first to dry-fry and the second to shallow-fry), and get the flatbreads cooking one immediately after the other – once you have started filling them, you need to fry them as quickly as possible before they start to go soggy.

SERVES 4 (MAKES 8)

sunflower oil, for frying
4 tablespoons plain live set yoghurt,
  to serve

Masala
4–6 fresh green chillies, seeds left in
6cm root ginger, peeled and
  roughly chopped
pinch of salt

Dough
360g chapatti flour, sieved
75ml sunflower oil, plus more
  for oiling

Filling
1 large red-skinned (or other waxy)
  potato, peeled
½ medium cauliflower
2 handfuls of fresh coriander,
  finely chopped
1½ teaspoons salt

Crush the chillies and ginger together with a pinch of salt using a pestle and mortar (or a blender), to make a fine masala paste.

Put the chapatti flour and oil into a large bowl and stir in 200ml of boiling water. Once it is cool enough to handle, knead the dough until it comes together and firms up. I usually knead for about 3 minutes – the longer you knead, the fluffier the finished flatbread will be. Smooth the surface of the dough with lightly oiled hands, then set aside.

Grate the potato into another large bowl, making the strands as long as possible. Grate the cauliflower into the same bowl and then add the masala paste, chopped coriander and salt. Mix with a light touch, tossing everything together to ensure that the vegetables are coated in the masala but without breaking up the potato strands.

Divide the dough into 16 roughly equal pieces, form them into balls between your palms and squash to flatten slightly. Place one of the flattened dough balls on a lightly floured work surface and roll it into a disc about 18cm in diameter (see method on page 91). Repeat with the remaining dough balls, placing the discs on a floured baking sheet as you go, making sure they don't overlap.

Put one of the chapatti discs back on the work surface. Take an eighth of the potato mixture and spread it evenly across the centre of the chapatti, leaving 1cm clear around the edge. Cover with a second chapatti and press down hard with your fingers to seal the edges – the dough should be sticky enough to seal the *paratha*.

Place 2 frying pans over a low heat. Dry-fry the *paratha* in the first frying pan for a minute on each side. In the meantime, fill and seal a second *paratha*. Heat 2 teaspoons of oil in the second frying pan and place the dry-fried *paratha* in it. Shallow-fry for a minute or so on each side, until crisp and golden brown. While the first *paratha* is frying in the oil, you can start dry-frying the second one and filling and sealing the third.

Remove the first *paratha* (now fried) from the pan and place on kitchen paper, then start shallow-frying the second one, put the third on to dry-fry and fill and seal the fourth. This is easier than it sounds, but if you think it all seems too complicated, simply cook one *paratha* at a time. Continue until all 8 have been cooked.

Serve 2 freshly cooked *parathas* per person, with a tablespoon of yoghurt to dip them into, *keri attana* pickle (page 194) to accompany them and a fresh mug of hot *adhu vari chai* (page 228).

Tikki puri –
Spicy fried dough puffs

(V, N)

*This is the perfect mid-morning snack to accompany a hot cup of tea.
My son Bobby goes crazy for* tikki puri *– he just can't stop eating them. I warn you –
they look and sound so simple, but they are very tasty and very, very moreish …*

sunflower oil, for frying

Masala
3–5 fresh green chillies, seeds left in
3–4 cloves of garlic
pinch of salt

Dough
340g chapatti flour, sieved
150ml sunflower oil
½ teaspoon turmeric
1 teaspoon salt
1 teaspoon carom seeds
1½ teaspoons cumin seeds,
  roasted* and crushed
1 teaspoon sugar

* SEE TOP TIPS (PAGE 26)
FOR HOW TO ROAST
CUMIN SEEDS.

Crush the chillies and garlic together with a pinch of salt using a pestle and mortar (or a blender), to make a fine masala paste.

Put all the dough ingredients into a large bowl. Add the masala paste and use your hands to combine. Pour in 150ml of warm water and mix until the dough comes together, then knead until firm and well worked. This dough is quite stiff, so you will need to really work it.

Divide the dough into 40 roughly equal pieces. Form the dough pieces into balls between your palms and squash to flatten slightly. Place one of the flattened dough balls on a lightly oiled work surface and roll into a disc about 6cm in diameter and roughly 5mm thick (see method on page 91). Repeat with the remaining dough balls, placing the *puri* discs on a lightly oiled baking sheet as you go, making sure they don't overlap.

Heat the frying oil – about 15cm deep – in a large pan over a high heat (or in a deep fat fryer, if you have one). Test the temperature by dropping a few little pieces of dough into the oil – when it is hot enough, they will float to the surface. Reduce the heat to medium.

Gently place the *puri* one by one in the oil – I tend to fry around 4 at a time, but it depends on the size of your pan. The *puri* will sink to the bottom of the pan initially, and float up after about 10 seconds. Fry for about 90 seconds, until crispy and full of air, using a wooden spoon to move them around and turn them so that they cook evenly. Remove from the oil with a slotted spoon and leave to rest on kitchen paper while you fry the next batch. Repeat until all the *puri* have been fried.

Serve while still hot and crispy, with a spoonful or two of *murabho* pickle (page 197) or *lila dhania lasan* relish (page 203) on the side and a nice hot cup of *adhu vari chai* (page 228).

Bhel ~
Crispy puffed rice, potato, chickpea, chapatti and chutney chaat

(V)

Bhel – difficult to describe, easy to love! Long before we opened the deli, I would make bhel *as a family snack at weekends, and Bobby would say that if only other people could taste it, it would wow the world. So obviously, once we started our streetside menu, we knew* bhel *would have to feature. Once you have fried the chapatti pieces and assembled the other ingredients, this dish is very quick to put together and should be served as soon as possible after combining. There is plenty of room for personal variation both in how you combine the ingredients and in finishing touches – in my family, Minal adds extra* lasan *chutney while Bobby likes to drench his in* imli *chutney. This recipe makes 4 generous servings, with a little left over for experimenting with different flavour combinations.*

SERVES 4

1 large red-skinned
  (or other waxy) potato
1 x 400g tin of chickpeas, rinsed
  and drained
1 medium green (unripe) mango,
  finely diced
1 medium red onion, finely diced
100g chapatti flour
2 teaspoons sunflower oil,
  plus more for frying
2 teaspoons lemon juice
¼ teaspoon salt
500g red-skinned (unroasted,
  unsalted) peanuts
250g *sev momra* (Indian vermicelli
  and puffed rice)
3 tablespoons *lila dhania lasan*
  (page 203), plus more to serve
3 tablespoons *lasan* chutney
  (page 209), plus more to serve
12 tablespoons *imli* chutney
  (page 210), plus more to serve
2 handfuls of fresh coriander,
  finely chopped

Boil the potato in its skin for 40 minutes or so, until a knife tip will slide in easily, then peel and cut into 1cm cubes. Put the potato cubes, chickpeas, mango and onion into separate small bowls close to hand, so that you can assemble the dish easily once you've finished frying.

Mix the flour, oil, lemon juice, salt and 40ml of warm water in a medium bowl until combined, then knead well until you have a firm dough. Smooth the surface with lightly oiled hands and leave to rest for 15 minutes.

Divide the dough in two. Form one half into a ball and roll out on a lightly floured work surface until about 2mm thick. Use a palette knife to cut into rectangles roughly 2 x 1cm, placing them on a lightly oiled tray as you go. Repeat with the other half of the dough.

Heat the frying oil – about 15cm deep – in a large pan over a high heat (or in a deep fat fryer, if you have one). Test the temperature by dropping a couple of pieces of dough into the oil – when it is hot enough, they will float to the surface. Reduce the heat to medium.

Using a slotted spoon, transfer 2 spoonfuls of dough pieces to the oil and use a wooden spoon to move them around so that they cook evenly. Fry for about 90 seconds, or until they start to turn golden brown. Remove from the oil with the slotted spoon and leave to rest on kitchen paper while you fry the next batch. Repeat until all the pieces have been fried.

Reduce the heat under the oil to low and add the peanuts. Fry for 2 minutes, gently stirring, until they have cracked slightly. Remove from the oil with a slotted spoon and leave to rest on kitchen paper for a minute. Put the *sev momra* into a large bowl, tip in the peanuts and mix to combine.

Put the *lila dhania lasan* and the *lasan* chutney into 2 separate small bowls. Add 1 tablespoon of cold water to each and stir.

Assemble the *bhel* in 4 wide bowls, using your hands to layer the dry ingredients. Start with a couple of handfuls of *sev momra* and peanuts in each bowl, and follow with a handful of potato cubes, a handful of chickpeas, a handful of chopped onion and half a handful of mango pieces. Top each serving with 3 tablespoons of *imli* chutney and a tablespoon each of the *lila dhania lasan* and *lasan* chutney. Divide half the coriander between the 4 bowls and mix gently but thoroughly to combine, making sure everything gets a good coating of chutney.

Garnish the bowls with the remaining coriander and serve immediately, with more chutney on the side for anyone who wants to add a little extra something to their dish.

VARIATION – DRY-FRIED PURI AND PEANUTS

If you are looking for a healthier option to deep-frying, you can dry-fry the dough. Roll half of it out into a disc and place it in a non-stick frying pan or on a *tawa* over a medium heat. Dry-fry for 2–3 minutes on each side until crisp, pressing down with a heatproof spatula while it cooks to remove any air. Remove from the pan and leave to rest on kitchen paper while you roll out and dry-fry the other half of the dough. Once cooled, break the discs into small pieces (roughly 2 x 1cm) to use in your *bhel*.

Dry-fry the peanuts for 5 minutes over a medium heat, stirring gently, until they start to crack, then remove from the pan and leave to rest on kitchen paper for a minute before mixing with the *sev momra*.

Bataka pauwa – Flattened rice with peanuts and potato

(V, WF, HO)

Flakes of flattened or beaten rice (pauwa) are often used in Indian cooking as a convenience food, and can be soaked, steamed, baked, fried or even made into porridge. You can find flattened rice in Indian supermarkets and online. This is a great quick-and-easy dish, something I can make with no planning or advance preparation from ingredients that are always in my fridge and store cupboard. So it's perfect for unexpected lunch guests.

SERVES 4

250g medium-thick flattened rice
130ml sunflower oil
1 teaspoon cumin seeds
½ teaspoon brown mustard seeds
15 fresh curry leaves
1 large red-skinned (or other waxy) potato, cut into 1cm chunks
½ teaspoon turmeric
1 teaspoon salt
4 teaspoons sesame seeds
100g red-skinned (unroasted, unsalted) peanuts
2 teaspoons sugar
2 handfuls of fresh coriander, finely chopped
2 tablespoons fresh lemon juice

Masala

2–3 fresh green chillies, seeds left in
1–2 cloves of garlic
4cm root ginger, peeled and roughly chopped
pinch of salt

Crush the chillies, garlic and ginger together with a pinch of salt using a pestle and mortar (or a blender), to make a fine masala paste.

Soak the rice for a minute in enough warm water to cover it, then drain.

Heat the oil in a wok or large frying pan over a medium heat and fry the cumin seeds until they start to darken. Tip in the mustard seeds and once they start to pop, carefully add the curry leaves – do this carefully, as the leaves will immediately start to sizzle and the oil may spit. Stir together, reduce the heat to low and stir in the potatoes, turmeric and salt. Turn the heat up slightly, cover and cook for 3–4 minutes, stirring occasionally, until the potatoes start to soften.

Stir in the masala paste, sesame seeds, peanuts, sugar and half the chopped coriander, then cover and leave to cook for 4–5 minutes over a low heat, until the potatoes are cooked through.

Add the drained rice and 2 tablespoons of warm water and stir gently – the *pauwa* will start to turn the yellow colour of the turmeric. Cover and cook for a further couple of minutes, stirring occasionally to stop anything sticking to the pan. Stir in the lemon juice and continue to cook, covered, until the *pauwa* has absorbed all the liquid and the dish has a loose rice-like texture.

Sprinkle with the remaining coriander and serve piping hot, with a cup of *adhu vari chai* (page 228).

MAIN DISHES

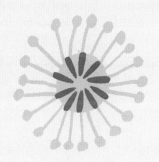

MAIN DISHES

Many of these dishes have their origins in traditional home cooking from Gujarat, Punjab and southern India, although they all have a little Kaushy twist! Some were taught to me as a child by my grandmother, while others were created by me here in northern England, inspired by meals with friends and family or by delicious discoveries made while travelling in India.

In the Gujarati recipes, such as wedding-favourite aubergine *renghan bataka*, garlicky purple yam *ratalu* or fresh green *wattana* and flower, with its sweet tender peas and cauliflower, you'll often find a little sugar or jaggery added. This is partly to appeal to the famous Gujarati sweet tooth, and partly to temper the chillies and balance any saltiness in order to produce harmonious flavours.

The dishes from Punjab tend to be rich and more strongly spiced – try fragrant, cinnamon-tomato chickpea *chole* or classic cauliflower and potato *aloo gobi*. Southern Indian cuisine by contrast is more rice-based, so it is no surprise that its most famous dish – *masala dosa* – consists of a lovely crispy rice and *dhal* pancake, filled with warming potato and coconut curry.

Most of these recipes have one or two vegetables as their stars. Some of these are familiar, like aubergines, potatoes, cauliflower, peas, tomatoes and mushrooms, while others may be less so, more exotic-sounding. These are the vegetables of my childhood: sweet purple yams, Indian broad beans, green cluster beans, violet-coloured hyacinth beans, bottle and ivy gourds, even green bananas. You'll also find recipes based around protein-rich pulses – chickpeas and lentils of many types – and firm, delicately flavoured *paneer* cheese.

Some main dishes are relatively dry in texture, making them easy to pick up with your fingers or scoop on to pieces of fresh *rotli*, *paratha* or sweet *mal pura* flatbread, while others have smooth spicy tomato or rich peanut satay sauces to soak into the fluffy rice that accompanies every meal in our household.

Wherever the dish comes from and whichever ingredient takes the starring role, I hope that the array of colours, textures and spices, along with the carefully crafted balance of sour, salty, spicy and sweet flavours, will excite your appetite and keep you and your guests coming back for more!

MAIN DISHES

Renghan reveya – Round aubergine satay

(V, WF, OG, HO)

I made this dish for my first ever cooking competition. I won, and as a result we got a great write-up in the local paper – I believe that was when things really started happening for the Prashad restaurant. I use round baby aubergines for this recipe, as they have a lovely firm texture and relatively few seeds, but you can use normal baby aubergines if you can't get hold of round ones.

SERVES 4

150g red-skinned (unroasted, unsalted) peanuts, finely chopped or blended

25g jaggery, cut into thin flakes (or demerara/soft brown sugar)

3 tablespoons ground coriander

2 teaspoons turmeric

1¼ teaspoons salt

1 teaspoon cumin seeds

¼ teaspoon asafetida

1 large tomato, finely chopped or blended

4cm root ginger, peeled and roughly chopped

2–3 teaspoons medium red chilli powder

2 handfuls of fresh coriander, finely chopped

150ml sunflower oil

16 round baby aubergines

Put the peanuts, jaggery, ground coriander, turmeric, salt, cumin seeds, asafetida and tomato into a large bowl. Mix together using your hands, then leave to rest for a few minutes to allow the spices to infuse.

Crush the ginger using a pestle and mortar (or a blender), to make a fine pulp. Stir the ginger, chilli powder, chopped coriander and oil into the peanut/tomato mixture and mix thoroughly to distribute the spices evenly through the marinade.

Cut the aubergines into quarters, leaving the last couple of centimetres at the stem end intact to hold them together. Gently open the aubergines out and spread a generous quantity of marinade on the cut surfaces. Be sure to spread it right to the end of the incisions, but take care not to overfill them or the aubergines may split apart completely – part of the beauty of this dish is that they are served whole.

Arrange the filled aubergines in a large pan and cover with any remaining marinade. Cover the pan and cook over a low heat for 5 minutes, then carefully pour 350ml of boiling water around the aubergines (don't pour it over them or you'll wash away the marinade). Cover the pan again and cook over a high heat for 2 minutes, or until the mixture comes to the boil. Reduce the heat to low and leave to simmer for about 25 minutes, or until tender (a knife tip should slide easily into the aubergines). Remove from the heat and leave to rest, covered, for at least 20 minutes to allow the flavours to infuse and the oil to be released from the dish.

Reheat over a medium heat, gently stirring until piping hot. Serve 4 baby aubergines per person, along with a good helping of the thick marinade-sauce, fresh *rotli* (page 170), *baath* (page 156) and *khudi* (page 193).

Renghan lilva –
Aubergine and Indian broad bean curry

(V, WF, N, HO)

Pea and bean dishes tend to be very popular at the restaurant, not least because sous chef Ramesh, manager Imran and my son Bobby all love them. Papdi lilva, also known as Indian broad or field beans, are rich in protein. They are available at Indian supermarkets and online, but if you can't get hold of any, substitute the same quantity of broad beans or edamame beans. This curry has a lovely texture, with a wonderful contrast between the softness of the aubergine and the firm bite of the papdi lilva.

SERVES 4

500g fresh *papdi lilva* (in pods),
  or 1 x 400g tin
100ml sunflower oil
1 teaspoon brown mustard seeds
2 teaspoons carom seeds
¼ teaspoon asafetida
3 medium aubergines,
  cut into 2cm cubes
2 teaspoons turmeric
1 tablespoon ground coriander
1¼ teaspoons salt
2 teaspoons sugar
2 handfuls of fresh coriander,
  finely chopped
2 medium tomatoes, roughly chopped

Masala
2–5 fresh green chillies, seeds left in
2–4 cloves of garlic
3cm root ginger, peeled and
  roughly chopped
pinch of salt

If using fresh *papdi lilva*, pod the beans, then rinse and drain. If using tinned ones, rinse twice in warm water, then drain.

Crush the chillies, garlic and ginger together with a pinch of salt using a pestle and mortar (or a blender), to make a fine masala paste.

Heat the oil in a large pan for about 90 seconds over a medium heat, then add the mustard seeds. When they start to pop, add the carom seeds and reduce the heat to low. Add the asafetida, masala paste, *papdi lilva*, aubergines, turmeric, ground coriander, salt and sugar and stir gently. Increase the heat to medium, stir in half the chopped coriander and 300ml of boiling water, then cover the pan and bring the mixture to the boil.

Reduce the heat to low, simmer for 5–6 minutes, then stir in the tomatoes and the remaining chopped coriander. Cover the pan again and cook for a further 5 minutes, then remove from the heat. Set aside to rest (still covered) for at least 10 minutes to allow the flavours to infuse.

When you are ready to eat, reheat over a medium heat until piping hot and serve with *baath* (page 156) and *dhal* (page 192), or try it with *baath*, *velmi* (page 182), *khudi* (page 193) and *methi safarjan* (page 202).

Renghan bataka –
Aubergine and potato curry
(V, WF, OG, N, HO)

We Gujaratis love aubergines, so at every Gujarati wedding feast you will find at least one renghan dish. This is a particular favourite. I remember once cooking it for 2,000 wedding guests – my husband had to prepare 140 kilos of aubergines! I like to use Kenyan aubergines for this recipe (and for Indian dishes in general) because they have a firm texture and keep their structure when cooked.

SERVES 4

75ml sunflower oil
1 teaspoon cumin seeds
1 teaspoon brown mustard seeds
¼ teaspoon asafetida
2 medium aubergines,
  cut into 2cm cubes
2 medium red-skinned (or other
  waxy) potatoes, peeled and cut into
  2cm cubes
1½ teaspoons turmeric
1½ teaspoons salt
½ teaspoon medium red chilli powder
2 teaspoons sugar
3 tablespoons ground coriander
½ teaspoon ground cumin
2 medium tomatoes, roughly chopped
2 handfuls of fresh coriander,
  coarsely chopped

Masala
3–6 medium fresh green chillies,
  seeds left in
3cm root ginger, peeled and
  roughly chopped
pinch of salt

Crush the chillies and ginger together with a pinch of salt using a pestle and mortar (or a blender), to make a fine masala paste.

Heat the oil in a large pan for a minute over a medium heat, then add the cumin and mustard seeds. When the mustard seeds start to pop, remove from the heat. Immediately add the asafetida, aubergines and potatoes, stir, then return to the heat. Stir in the masala paste, turmeric, salt, chilli powder, sugar, ground coriander, ground cumin and 150ml of boiling water, then cook covered for 3–4 minutes over a low heat. Increase the heat to bring to a simmering boil, then simmer uncovered over a low heat again for 5–6 minutes, stirring occasionally.

Stir in the tomatoes and half the fresh coriander, then cover the pan and simmer for a further 5 minutes, or until the potatoes are cooked through. Remove from the heat and leave to rest, covered, for at least 10 minutes to enable the spices to infuse and the flavours to develop.

Gently reheat over a low heat and bring to a simmering boil. Sprinkle with the remaining chopped coriander and serve piping hot with *rotli* (page 170), *tuvar dhal kichdi* (page 168) and *khudi* (page 193).

Bombay bataka –
Tamarind, tomato and potato curry

(V, WF, OG, N, HO)

This dish featured on Prashad's very first menu and is our take on traditional Bombay potatoes. One of my regular customers at the restaurant ordered a portion of this every week for over a year, declaring it to be the best curry she had ever had!

SERVES 4

3 medium red-skinned (or other waxy) potatoes

25g dried tamarind (from a block)

3cm root ginger, peeled and roughly chopped

75ml sunflower oil

2–4 dried red chillies, snapped in half

1 teaspoon cumin seeds

1 teaspoon brown mustard seeds

¼ teaspoon asafetida

1 x 400g tin of peeled plum tomatoes, finely chopped or blended

25g jaggery, cut into thin flakes (or demerara/soft brown sugar)

1 teaspoon medium red chilli powder

1 tablespoon ground coriander

1½ teaspoons turmeric

1¼ teaspoons salt

2 handfuls of fresh coriander, finely chopped

¾ teaspoon *garam masala*

Boil the potatoes in their skins for 40 minutes or so, until a knife tip will slide in easily, then peel and cut into 2cm cubes. Soak the dried tamarind in 200ml of boiling water for 10 minutes, then pulp with your fingers and sieve into a small bowl. Crush the ginger using a pestle and mortar (or a blender), to make a fine pulp.

Heat the oil in a large pan for a minute over a medium heat and add the dried red chillies, cumin seeds and mustard seeds. When the mustard seeds start to pop, reduce the heat to low and stir in the asafetida, tomatoes and jaggery. Stir over a low heat for a minute or so, until the jaggery has dissolved.

Increase the heat to high and stir in the tamarind water, crushed ginger, chilli powder, ground coriander, turmeric, salt, half the fresh coriander and 400ml of boiling water. Cover and cook for 10 minutes to bring the spices together and intensify the flavours.

Add the *garam masala* and stir well – this is a strong flavour and needs to be thoroughly mixed in before you add the dish's main ingredient. Stir in the potatoes gently to avoid breaking them up, then remove the pan from the heat, sprinkle with the remaining chopped coriander and leave to rest, covered, for at least 10 minutes to allow the flavours to infuse.

Reheat over a medium heat until piping hot and serve with *puri* (page 177) and *kakadhi raitu* (page 212), or with *rotli* (page 170) and *sing dhania* dip (page 215).

Ferar bataka –
Ginger-chilli peanuts and potatoes

(WF, OG, HO)

'Ferar' means 'suitable for fasting'. Gujarati culture has many fasting days – these may be either festivals or days on which you are specifically advised by the priest to fast, depending on your date and time of birth. Fasting lasts from sunrise to sunset and you can only eat once during the day – most people choose to eat in the evening, after work. This is my favourite 'break-fasting' dish, and my daughter-in-law Minal likes it so much that she makes it even when we are not fasting.

SERVES 4

4 medium red-skinned
  (or other waxy) potatoes
5cm root ginger, peeled and
  roughly chopped
6–8 fresh green chillies, seeds left in
100g unsalted butter
80g red-skinned (unroasted,
  unsalted) peanuts, coarsely chopped
  or blended
1½ teaspoons rock salt, ground
  (or unrefined sea salt, if you're
  not fasting)
1 teaspoon sugar
1 lemon, quartered, to serve

Boil the potatoes in their skins for 40 minutes or so, until a knife tip will slide in easily, then peel and cut into 1.5cm cubes. Crush the ginger using a pestle and mortar (or a blender), to make a fine pulp. Slice the chillies into fine rings.

Melt the butter in a large pan over a medium heat, then reduce the heat to low and stir in the ginger pulp and chilli rings. Continue to stir for a minute or two while the ginger cooks and the flavours infuse the butter, then stir in the peanuts. Increase the heat to low/medium, stir in the salt and sugar and fry the peanuts for a couple of minutes, stirring throughout. Gently stir in the potatoes until they are coated in the spiced butter, then cover the pan and leave to cook over a low heat for 2 minutes or so, until they are heated through.

Serve steaming hot, with a quarter of lemon for squeezing over the potatoes, along with *bhakri* (page 172) and *mura raitu* (page 212).

Sukhu bataka –
Spicy picnic potatoes

(V, WF, N, HO)

This is a traditional Patel family outing dish – whenever we went out for the day with the children when they were small, we'd include this in our picnic. It's filling, full of flavour and easy to eat, which makes it perfect for hungry children and husbands.

SERVES 4

4 medium red-skinned
 (or other waxy) potatoes
100ml sunflower oil
1½ teaspoons brown mustard seeds
¼ teaspoon asafetida
1 teaspoon salt
1 teaspoon turmeric
2–4 teaspoons ground coriander
½ teaspoon ground cumin
1 handful of fresh coriander,
 finely chopped

Masala
3–5 fresh green chillies, seeds left in
1–3 cloves of garlic
2cm root ginger, peeled and
 roughly chopped
pinch of salt

Boil the potatoes in their skins for 40 minutes or so, until a knife tip will slide in easily, then peel and cut into 1cm cubes. Crush the chillies, garlic and ginger together with a pinch of salt using a pestle and mortar (or a blender), to make a fine masala paste.

Heat the oil in a large lidded frying pan for 90 seconds over a medium heat, then add the mustard seeds. When they start to pop, reduce the heat to low and gently stir in the potatoes and asafetida. Add the salt and turmeric and continue to stir gently, coating the potatoes without breaking them.

Increase the heat to high, cover and cook for 3 minutes, stirring occasionally to stop the potatoes from sticking. Stir in the masala paste, ground coriander and ground cumin, reduce the heat to low, then cover the pan and cook for 5–6 minutes, stirring every so often, until the potato is cooked through.

Sprinkle with chopped coriander and serve hot with *puri* (page 177) and *keri attana* (page 194).

Aloo gobi –
Punjabi cauliflower and potato curry

(WF, N)

Aloo gobi is probably one of the best-known vegetarian Indian dishes and is a national favourite. You can find many different versions of this classic dish from the north-west of India, but this recipe is based on one given to me by a good friend, which I then modified and tweaked to add my own touch.

SERVES 4

2 medium red-skinned
  (or other waxy) potatoes
1 medium cauliflower
150ml sunflower oil
1½ teaspoons cumin seeds
¼ teaspoon asafetida
1 x 400g tin of peeled plum tomatoes,
  finely chopped or blended
1½ teaspoons turmeric
2–4 teaspoons ground coriander
½ teaspoon ground cumin
½ teaspoon medium red chilli powder
1 teaspoon salt
45g unsalted butter
2 handfuls of fresh coriander,
  finely chopped

Masala
4–6 fresh green chillies, seeds left in
3–6 cloves of garlic
4cm root ginger, peeled and
  roughly chopped
pinch of salt

Crush the chillies, garlic and ginger together with a pinch of salt using a pestle and mortar (or a blender), to make a fine masala paste. Peel the potatoes and cut into 3cm cubes. Cut the cauliflower (including 5mm of the stem) into small florets, each about 4cm long.

Heat the oil in a large pan for a minute over a medium heat. Tip in the cumin seeds and as soon as they start to brown, stir in the asafetida and reduce the heat to low. Add the potatoes and stir until they are coated in oil. Increase the heat to medium, then cover the pan and leave to cook for 3 minutes, stirring occasionally to prevent the potatoes sticking or scorching. Reduce the heat to low and cook for a further 3 minutes, stirring every so often.

Stir in the masala paste, tomatoes, turmeric, ground coriander, ground cumin, chilli powder, salt, butter and half the fresh coriander, mix well to distribute the spices and cook for 1 minute.

Stir in the cauliflower florets, increase the heat to medium, then cover the pan and cook for 3 minutes, stirring occasionally. Reduce the heat to low again and leave to cook, covered, for a further 10 minutes or so, until the potatoes are cooked through.

Remove from the heat, sprinkle with the remaining chopped coriander, then cover the pan again and leave to rest for at least 10 minutes, to let the flavours develop.

Reheat over a medium heat, stirring carefully so as not to break up the cauliflower. Once steaming hot again, serve with *paratha* (page 174), *masala kakadhi* (page 199) and *phudino dai* (page 211), or with *bhakri* (page 172), *chevti dhal* (page 126) and *murabho* (page 197), or alternatively with *baath* (page 156), *velmi* (page 182), *khudi* (page 193) and *methi safarjan* (page 202).

Wattana and flower –
Pea and cauliflower curry

(V, WF, OG, N, HO)

This dish appeared on the first restaurant menu at Prashad, and seven years on is still remembered fondly by my customers. The combination of cauliflower and peas is characteristic of traditional Gujarati cooking – we love good textures and a little sweetness in our cuisine. If you are using frozen peas, I recommend you use petits pois, *as they are smaller and sweeter than ordinary garden peas.*

SERVES 4

100ml sunflower oil
1 teaspoon cumin seeds
1 teaspoon brown mustard seeds
½ teaspoon asafetida
1 medium cauliflower,
  cut into 1cm pieces
1 teaspoon turmeric
1 tablespoon ground coriander
1½ teaspoons salt
1 teaspoon sugar
400g fresh or frozen peas
1 medium tomato, finely chopped
1 large handful of fresh coriander,
  roughly chopped

Masala
3–6 fresh green chillies, seeds left in
5cm root ginger, peeled and
  roughly chopped
pinch of salt

Crush the chillies and ginger together with a pinch of salt using a pestle and mortar (or a blender), to make a fine masala paste.

Heat the oil in a large thick-based frying pan over a medium heat for 30 seconds, then add the cumin and mustard seeds. When the mustard seeds start to pop, reduce the heat to low and stir in the asafetida. (Heating the spices in this order is essential to the flavour.)

Add the cauliflower, then return the heat to medium and stir in the masala paste, turmeric, ground coriander, salt and sugar, plus 75ml of boiling water (if using fresh peas – I find that frozen peas don't need it). Cover the pan and leave to cook for 8–10 minutes, stirring every few minutes. Stir in the peas and tomato, cover the pan again and cook for a further 3–5 minutes. Remove from the heat and sprinkle with the chopped coriander, then leave to rest, covered, for 5 minutes or so, to let the flavours develop.

Serve with *rotli* (page 170), *baath* (page 156) and *dhal* (page 192).

Makai ~
Corn-on-the-cob curry

(V, WF, N, HO)

This dish always reminds me of Bonfire Night – it became a tradition that we would eat it at a friend's bonfire party every year. I find that this dish works best using frozen corn-on-the-cob, but you can of course use fresh corn cobs if you have them. The sweetness from the corn and the caramelized onion balances the spices in a delicious way.

SERVES 4

4 frozen corn-on-the-cob
2 medium onions
175ml sunflower oil
1 x 400g tin of peeled plum
  tomatoes, finely chopped or blended
2 teaspoons salt
1 teaspoon medium red
  chilli powder
1½ teaspoons turmeric
2–4 teaspoons ground coriander
1 teaspoon ground cumin
2 handfuls of fresh coriander,
  finely chopped
1 teaspoon *garam masala*

Masala
2–4 fresh green chillies, seeds left in
8cm root ginger, peeled and
  roughly chopped
pinch of salt

Remove the frozen corn-on-the-cob from the freezer and let it start thawing at room temperature while you prepare the other ingredients.

Crush the chillies and ginger together with a pinch of salt using a pestle and mortar (or a blender), to make a fine masala paste. Finely chop or blend 1 onion to form a smooth paste and dice the other finely.

Heat the oil in a large pan (big enough to fit the corn cobs into) for 30 seconds over a medium/high heat, then stir in the onion paste. Cover and leave to fry gently for 3 minutes, until the paste is starting to brown, then stir in the diced onion. Cover the pan again, then reduce the heat to low and leave to cook for 2 minutes before stirring. Continue to cook, covered, stirring every couple of minutes, until the onions have caramelized to a lovely dark brown. It's important to brown them slowly like this, taking care not to burn them, as they give the dish its rich colour and a sweetness that marries beautifully with the intense spices.

Add the masala paste, tomatoes, salt, chilli powder, turmeric, ground coriander, ground cumin and half the fresh coriander and mix thoroughly to combine. Cover and leave to cook for 2 minutes, then stir in 750ml of boiling water.

If the corn cobs have been frozen whole, cut them in half across the middle (or in thirds if you prefer). Gently place in the onion/tomato mixture and stir to coat in the sauce. Bring to the boil over a high heat, then reduce to medium, cover and leave to simmer for 20 minutes. Check to see whether the corn is soft and fully cooked – if not, reduce the heat to low and cook for a further 5 minutes or so.

Remove from the heat and carefully stir in the *garam masala*, and the other handful of coriander. cover and leave to rest for at least 20 minutes to let the flavours develop.

Reheat over a medium heat and serve steaming hot, with generous quantities of the thick rich sauce spooned over each helping, accompanied by fresh *rotli* (page 170) and *phudino kandha* (page 211).

Ghuvar –
Carom, onion and green cluster bean curry

(V, WF, N, HO)

Back in the early sixties, when my husband and I were first settling in the UK, I couldn't cook this for him even though it was one of his favourite dishes, as we just couldn't afford to buy green cluster beans. He loves his lilotri *(green veg), but life was all about potatoes and pulses then. Green cluster beans are related to French and string beans (which you can use if you can't find any* ghuvar*), although cluster beans are paler, flatter and more fibrous. They can also be slightly bitter sometimes, so I add a little sugar to this curry to balance the flavour.*

SERVES 4

500g *ghuvar* (green cluster beans)
150ml sunflower oil
2 teaspoons carom seeds
¼ teaspoon asafetida
1 medium onion, chopped or
  blended to a smooth paste
1¾ teaspoons salt
2 teaspoons turmeric
1 tablespoon ground coriander
½ teaspoon ground cumin
2 teaspoons sugar
1 large tomato, finely chopped
  or blended
1 handful of fresh coriander,
  finely chopped

Masala
2–4 fresh green chillies, seeds left in
5cm root ginger, peeled and
  roughly chopped
pinch of salt

Crush the chillies and ginger together with a pinch of salt using a pestle and mortar (or a blender), to make a fine masala paste.

Top and tail the beans by snapping about 3mm off each end, then cut them in half across the middle.

Heat the oil in a large pan for 90 seconds over a medium heat, then add the carom seeds, quickly followed by the asafetida and then the onion paste – carom seeds are strongly flavoured, so don't fry them on their own for more than a few seconds. Once the onion paste is sizzling, cover the pan and cook for about 5 minutes, checking and stirring at regular intervals, until the paste is golden brown.

Stir in the cluster beans and reduce the heat to low. Stir in the masala paste, salt, turmeric, ground coriander, ground cumin and sugar, then pour in 150ml of boiling water. Increase the heat to bring back to the boil, then cover and simmer over a low heat for 4–5 minutes, stirring occasionally to make sure nothing sticks to the bottom of the pan.

Stir in the chopped tomato and coriander, cover the pan again, and leave to cook for a further 15 minutes, or until the beans are cooked through. Remove from the heat and leave to rest, covered, for at least 15 minutes to let the flavours develop.

Reheat over a low heat until piping hot, and serve with *mung dhal kichdi* (page 167) and *khudi* (page 193).

Sukhu bhinda bataka ~
Mustard seed, okra and potato curry

(V, WF, N, HO)

Before we opened Prashad, my husband would always look forward to our family get-together meals on Sundays. These days Minal and Bobby work at the restaurant on Sundays, but this is still one of my all-time favourite family dinner curries. It's a special dish that sets the tone for a great feast. As with bhinda *(page 134), you need to start preparing this dish the day before you want to cook it.*

SERVES 4

650g okra
2 medium red-skinned
 (or other waxy) potatoes
125ml sunflower oil
1½ teaspoons fenugreek seeds
½ teaspoon brown mustard seeds
¼ teaspoon asafetida
2 teaspoons salt
1½ teaspoons turmeric
2–4 teaspoons ground coriander
½ teaspoon ground cumin
½ teaspoon medium red chilli powder
1 handful of fresh coriander,
 finely chopped

Masala
4–6 fresh green chillies,
 seeds left in
3–4 cloves of garlic
pinch of salt

Wash and carefully dry the okra. Trim the tops, cut in half lengthways, then cut each piece into 3 chunks (each about 2cm long). Spread out on a baking tray and leave uncovered to oxidize and dry for about 24 hours.

Crush the chillies and garlic together with a pinch of salt using a pestle and mortar (or a blender), to make a fine masala paste.

Peel the potatoes and cut into chunks roughly 1 x 4cm.

Heat the oil in a large frying pan for about 1 minute over a medium heat, then add the fenugreek and mustard seeds. When the mustard seeds start to pop, stir in the asafetida and potatoes, ensuring that the potatoes are well coated in oil. Increase the heat to high and fry for 1 minute, then stir in the okra and return the heat to medium.

Gently stir in the salt and turmeric, then cover the pan and leave to cook for 3 minutes. Add the masala paste, ground coriander, ground cumin and chilli powder and stir gently to mix, being careful not to break the delicate okra. Cover and leave to cook for 5 minutes, or until the potatoes are cooked through. Stir once more, then remove the pan from the heat and leave to rest, covered, for about 5 minutes to allow the flavours to infuse.

Reheat over a low heat until piping hot, then sprinkle with the chopped coriander and serve with *khudi* (page 193), *mung dhal kichdi* (page 167), *juvar na rotla* (page 173) and *keri attana* (page 194). Alternatively, if you are in a celebratory mood, serve with *rotli* (page 170), *dhal* (page 192), *baath* (page 156), *kandha raitu* (page 212), *limbu attana* (page 196) and *rava no sehro* (page 234) for the full Patel family feast experience!

Chevti dhal –
Mixed lentil curry

(WF, N, HO)

During my housewife years, before Prashad, my husband insisted that we ate a lentil dish at least once a week. This is one of his favourites – simple, tasty and filling. The mixture of different dhals *gives a wonderful variety of colour, texture and flavour.*

SERVES 4

80g *chana dhal* (Bengal gram *dhal/* split skinned black chickpeas)
80g *mung dhal* (yellow split mung beans)
80g *urad dhal* (white lentils)
80g *masoor dhal* (split red lentils)
1 teaspoon sunflower oil, plus 75ml for frying the spices
1–3 medium fresh green chillies
1 teaspoon cumin seeds
½ teaspoon brown mustard seeds
¼ teaspoon asafetida
¾ teaspoon turmeric
2–4 teaspoons ground coriander
½ teaspoon ground cumin
1½ teaspoons salt
2 handfuls of fresh coriander, finely chopped
50g unsalted butter

Masala
4–6 fresh green chillies, seeds left in
4–6 cloves of garlic
pinch of salt

Mix the *dhals* together, then rinse at least 4 times in warm water (see page 25) and drain.

Crush the chillies and garlic together with a pinch of salt using a pestle and mortar (or a blender), to make a fine masala paste.

Put the *dhals* into a large pan with 900ml of boiling water. Bring to the boil, then simmer over a medium heat for a couple of minutes until it starts to foam. Skim the froth from the surface, add the teaspoon of oil, then reduce the heat to low/medium and simmer three-quarters covered for a further 25–30 minutes, stirring occasionally and checking them after 25 minutes. Add another 50ml of boiling water if the *dhals* start to look dry. When they are soft and cooked through, remove the pan from the heat and set aside, but do not drain.

Slice the fresh chilli(es) in half lengthways and remove the seeds, then cut each piece in half across the middle to produce chunks roughly 3–4cm long. Heat 75ml of oil in a large pan for a minute over a medium heat, then add the cumin seeds and mustard seeds. When the mustard seeds start to pop, stir in the asafetida and green chilli pieces and reduce the heat to low. Stir in the masala paste, turmeric, ground coriander, ground cumin, salt and half the fresh coriander and fry for 3 minutes, stirring constantly while the spices infuse the oil.

Stir in the *dhals* along with the water in which they were cooked, then pour in a further 200ml of boiling water if you like (it depends how liquid you like your *dhal*), stir, and cook uncovered for 3 minutes. Add the remaining chopped coriander and the butter and stir again. Remove from the heat and leave to rest, covered, for at least 10 minutes to allow the flavours to infuse.

Reheat over a medium heat and serve piping hot, with *bhakri* (page 172) and *kakadhi raitu* (page 212).

Valor ajmo –
Tomato, carom and hyacinth bean curry

(V, WF, N, HO)

I find I can buy fresh hyacinth beans (imported from India or Kenya) all year round at vegetable markets in Bradford, whereas in India they only grow immediately after the rainy season. The plants produce lovely fragrant flowers and beautiful purple pods, and hyacinth bean dishes are very popular at Gujarati weddings because they pair beautifully with the traditional wedding dessert shrikhand. *I recommend that you use fresh hyacinth beans (bought in the pods, which you also cook and eat) whenever possible; you need to be very careful if you use the dried beans, as they require prolonged boiling to remove any toxins.*

SERVES 4

500g fresh hyacinth beans
  (weight including pods)
100ml sunflower oil
½ teaspoon brown mustard seeds
2 teaspoons carom seeds
¼ teaspoon asafetida
2 teaspoons turmeric
1½ teaspoons salt
2–4 teaspoons ground coriander
½ teaspoon ground cumin
2 teaspoons sugar
1 large tomato, chopped or blended
  to a coarse pulp
2 handfuls of fresh coriander,
  finely chopped

Masala
4–6 fresh green chillies, seeds left in
1–3 cloves of garlic
3cm root ginger, peeled and
  roughly chopped
pinch of salt

Crush the chillies, garlic and ginger together with a pinch of salt using a pestle and mortar (or a blender), to make a fine masala paste.

Hyacinth beans are cooked in their opened pods (which are also eaten), so rinse the pods, remove the strings from along the seams, then split them open and cut them in half across the middle. (Check that there are no insects hiding inside.)

Heat the oil in a large pan for 90 seconds over a medium heat, then add the mustard seeds. When they start to pop, add the carom seeds and fry for 30 seconds, then add the asafetida and the hyacinth beans in their pods and reduce the heat to low. Add the masala paste, turmeric, salt, ground coriander, ground cumin and sugar, stir, and pour in 100ml of boiling water. Increase the heat to bring back to the boil, then stir again, cover the pan and simmer over a low heat for 5 minutes.

Stir in the tomato and half the fresh coriander, cover the pan again, and leave to cook for a further 8–10 minutes, or until the beans are cooked through. Remove from the heat, sprinkle with the remaining chopped coriander, and leave to rest, covered, for at least 10 minutes to allow the flavours to infuse.

Reheat over a low heat until piping hot, and serve with *bhakri* (page 172) and *mura raitu* (page 212).

Ghilora reveya –
Stuffed ivy gourd curry

(V, WF, N, HO)

Ivy gourd (ghilora) is also known by a variety of other names, including 'baby watermelon', 'little gourd' and even 'gentleman's toes'! It looks rather like a cucumber (it is from the same family) and its vines spread like wildfire, growing up to 10cm a day. Ghilora was my late father-in-law's absolute favourite vegetable; he would pick them fresh from the garden and I would help my mother-in-law to prepare this dish. Try to use slim gourds whenever possible, as plump ones may be overripe and red-fleshed when you cut into them.

SERVES 4

800g ivy gourds
100ml sunflower oil
2 medium tomatoes, chopped or
  blended to a smooth pulp
1 medium onion, chopped or
  blended to a fine paste
1½ teaspoons turmeric
1½ teaspoons salt
2–4 teaspoons ground coriander
½ teaspoon ground cumin
¼ teaspoon asafetida
½ teaspoon medium red
  chilli powder
1 teaspoon cumin seeds
1 teaspoon *garam masala*
1 teaspoon sugar
1 handful of fresh coriander,
  finely chopped

Masala
3–5 fresh green chillies, seeds left in
6cm root ginger, peeled and
  roughly chopped
pinch of salt

Wash the ivy gourds and cut them lengthways into quarters, leaving 1cm or so at the stem end intact to hold them together.

Crush the chillies and ginger together with a pinch of salt using a pestle and mortar (or in a blender) to make a fine masala paste. Put the masala paste and all the rest of the ingredients into a large bowl and mix together using your hands, then leave to rest for a few minutes to allow the flavours to infuse.

Gently open out the gourds and spread a generous quantity of marinade on the cut surfaces – the marinade will be quite runny, so don't worry if it oozes out a little. Be sure to spread it right to the end of the incisions, but take care not to split the gourds.

Place the stuffed gourds along with any leftover marinade in a large thick-based frying pan over a high heat and cook for a couple of minutes, stirring and gently lifting with a spatula to make sure they don't stick to the pan. Reduce the heat to medium, cover the pan and cook for 5 minutes, stirring gently every so often. Then reduce the heat to low and leave to cook, covered, for a further 15 minutes.

Carefully pour 150ml of boiling water around the gourds, then cover the pan again and cook for 7–8 minutes. Remove from the heat and leave to rest, covered, for at least 10 minutes to allow the flavours to infuse.

Reheat over a medium heat until steaming hot, and serve with *paratha* (page 174) and plenty of plain live set yoghurt to dollop on top.

Dhudhi chana –
Bottle gourd and split chickpea curry

(V, WF, N, HO)

The texture of this dish is magical – soft and silky – and the chana dhal *adds a sweet nutty flavour. Try a piece of gourd before you start cooking, and don't use it if it tastes bitter, as bitter gourd juice can sometimes cause stomach problems. If you can't find bottle gourd, use a small butternut squash instead.*

SERVES 4

300g *chana dhal* (Bengal gram *dhal/* split skinned black chickpeas)
150ml sunflower oil, plus 1 teaspoon
4 dried red chillies
½ teaspoon brown mustard seeds
2 teaspoons carom seeds
¼ teaspoon asafetida
1 medium bottle gourd, peeled and cut into 1.5cm cubes
1 teaspoon turmeric
2–4 teaspoons ground coriander
½ teaspoon ground cumin
1 teaspoon salt
2 teaspoons sugar
½ teaspoon *garam masala*
1 handful of fresh coriander, finely chopped

Masala
4–6 fresh green chillies, seeds left in
2–4 cloves of garlic
3cm root ginger, peeled and roughly chopped
pinch of salt

Rinse the *chana dhal* 3 times in warm water (see page 25), then put it into a large pan with 1 litre of boiling water. Bring to the boil over a high heat and cook for a couple of minutes, until it starts to foam. Skim the froth from the surface, add the teaspoon of oil and reduce the heat to medium. Simmer, three-quarters covered, for about 35–40 minutes, stirring occasionally and adding another 250ml of boiling water as and when needed to keep the *dhal* covered. When the *dhal* is soft and cooked through, drain and set aside.

Crush the chillies, garlic and ginger together with a pinch of salt using a pestle and mortar (or in a blender), to make a fine masala paste.

Heat the 150ml of oil in a large pan for 30 seconds over a medium heat, then add the dried red chillies. As soon as they start to brown, add the mustard seeds. When the mustard seeds start to pop, reduce the heat to low and add the carom seeds, asafetida and bottle gourd. Mix gently, then stir in the masala paste, turmeric, ground coriander, ground cumin, salt and sugar. Pour in 200ml of boiling water, stir, turn up the heat and bring to the boil. Cover and simmer over a medium heat for 10 minutes, stirring occasionally to make sure nothing sticks to the pan. Add another 100ml of boiling water, then cover the pan again and cook for a further 5 minutes, stirring every so often.

Add the *dhal* to the spiced bottle gourd, stir gently, and cook for 2 minutes over a medium heat. Remove from the heat, stir in the *garam masala*, sprinkle with the chopped coriander and leave to rest, covered, for at least 10 minutes to let the flavours develop.

Starches from the *dhal* will form a film over the top of the cooled curry, but this will disappear as you stir and reheat it over a medium heat. Once it is hot through, serve with *puri* (page 177) and *rai marcha* (page 198).

Desi chana –
Garlicky black chickpea and potato curry

(V, WF, N, HO)

My daughter Hina was only about four years old when we first ate this dish when visiting friends in Leeds. It was so delicious that I went straight home and created my own version. The dark brown outer skin of desi chana *(also called* kala chana *or brown chickpeas) is thicker than that of larger, lighter-coloured chickpeas, making them higher in fibre and better for those wanting to regulate their blood sugar. Tinned* desi chana *are available in supermarkets, Indian food stores and online, but if you don't have any, this recipe works very well with ordinary tinned chickpeas too.*

SERVES 4

1 large red-skinned (or other
  waxy) potato
150ml sunflower oil
2 teaspoons cumin seeds
1 handful of fresh coriander,
  finely chopped
1¼ teaspoons salt
2–4 teaspoons ground coriander
½ teaspoon ground cumin
½ teaspoon *garam masala*
1½ teaspoons turmeric
3 x 400g tins of *desi chana*
  (black chickpeas), rinsed and drained
1 lemon, quartered, to serve

Masala
3–5 fresh green chillies, seeds left in
4–6 cloves of garlic
3cm root ginger, peeled and
  roughly chopped
pinch of salt

Boil the potato in its skin for 40 minutes or so, until a knife tip will slide in easily, then peel, cut into 2cm cubes and leave to cool.

Crush the chillies, garlic and ginger together with a pinch of salt using a pestle and mortar (or a blender), to make a fine masala paste.

Heat the oil in a large pan for 1 minute over a medium heat, then add the cumin seeds. Fry until they start to brown – this should take less than a minute, so be careful not to overcook or burn them – then reduce the heat to low.

Add the masala paste, fresh coriander, salt, ground coriander, ground cumin, *garam masala* and turmeric, mix well to combine and cook for a couple of minutes. Stir in the *desi chana*, cover and leave to cook for 5 minutes. Resist the temptation to remove the lid to check on it during this time, as you want the spices to intensify and infuse the chickpeas.

Gently fold in the potatoes, taking care not to break them up. Cover and cook for a further 5 minutes, stirring occasionally to make sure nothing is sticking or scorching.

Serve steaming hot, on a bed of *baath* (page 156), with *sing dhania* dip (page 215) and a lemon quarter on the side for squeezing over and to add a little citrus kick.

Chole –
Cinnamon-spice chickpea curry

(V, WF, N, HO)

*Chole is famous the world over. It is enjoyed at different times of the day throughout
South Asia: in Lahore it is eaten for breakfast; in Punjab, it is served as a snack and referred
to as* chaat; *in Gujarat it is treated as a main meal and eaten with* bathura. *It is also the dish that
first persuaded Gordon Ramsay that we could be Britain's Best Restaurant! Chole is simple
to make, and the focus is really on the balance of spices. The spice preparations make all the
difference to the flavours of the finished dish – for example, the cumin cooked with the onion
forms a base note, while the cumin in the* garam masala *creates an upper flavour, together
building delicious layers.*

3 x 400g tins of chickpeas, rinsed
  and drained
4 teaspoons sunflower oil,
  plus 75ml
15g coriander seeds
1 cinnamon stick (7–8cm long)
3–6 dried red chillies
8 cloves
1 teaspoon black peppercorns
6 dried Indian bay leaves
2 teaspoons cumin seeds
1 medium onion, chopped
  or blended to a smooth paste
4cm root ginger, peeled and
  roughly chopped
1 x 400g tin of peeled plum tomatoes,
  finely chopped or blended
1¾ teaspoons salt
1 teaspoon medium red chilli powder
1 teaspoon turmeric
1 teaspoon sugar
2 handfuls of fresh coriander,
  finely chopped

Place the chickpeas in a large pan with 500ml of warm water and boil for about 5 minutes over a high heat. Remove from the heat and set aside, still in their cooking water.

Heat 4 teaspoons of oil in a small pan for 30 seconds over a low heat, then stir in the coriander seeds, cinnamon, red chillies, cloves, peppercorns, bay leaves and 1 teaspoon of the cumin seeds. Fry the spices for 5 minutes or so, until dark brown, stirring continuously so that they don't burn, then set this *garam masala* aside to cool.

Heat the remaining 75ml of oil in a large pan for a minute over a medium heat, then add the other teaspoon of cumin seeds and fry until they start to brown. This only takes a minute or two, so be careful not to overcook or burn them. Stir the onion paste into the cumin seeds (watch out, as the oil may spit) and fry until dark brown, stirring regularly to avoid sticking or burning – I usually stir, cover the pan, and leave the mixture to cook for a minute before stirring again, repeating this 5 or 6 times until the onion is done.

Crush the ginger using a pestle and mortar (or a blender), to make a fine pulp. Stir the tomatoes into the onions, followed by the ginger, salt, red chilli powder, turmeric and sugar, then increase the heat to high. Stir in the chickpeas with their cooking water, along with an additional 300ml of warm water, then cover the pan and leave to simmer for 5 minutes, stirring occasionally.

While the chickpeas are cooking, finely grind the cooled roasted spices in a blender or with a pestle and mortar. Add to the chickpea mixture, stir, then remove the pan from the heat.

Sprinkle with the chopped coriander, then cover the pan again and leave to rest for around 10 minutes to allow the flavours to infuse.

Reheat over a medium heat until piping hot, and serve with *bathura* (page 178), *jeera baath* (page 158) and *phudino kandha* (page 211).

Bhinda –
Fenugreek, tomato and okra curry

(V, WF, N, HO)

This is a dish with complex flavours that requires exact timings to ensure the correct balance. We cooked it in the finals of Gordon Ramsay's Best Restaurant competition because Bobby wanted to show that we could push ourselves and showcase a delicious but unusual dish. The main trick to cooking okra is to stop it becoming too slimy, which we do here by drying it for 24 hours before cooking – so you need to start preparing this dish the day before you want to make it.

SERVES 4

800g okra
175ml sunflower oil
1 teaspoon fenugreek seeds
1 teaspoon brown mustard seeds
¼ teaspoon asafetida
1 x 400g tin of peeled plum
  tomatoes, finely chopped or blended
1¼ teaspoons salt
1¼ teaspoons turmeric
2–4 teaspoons ground coriander
½ teaspoon ground cumin
2 handfuls of fresh coriander,
  finely chopped

Masala
3–4 fresh green chillies, seeds left in
3–4 cloves of garlic
pinch of salt

Wash and carefully dry the okra. Trim the tops, cut into 1cm chunks, spread out on a baking tray and leave uncovered to oxidize and dry for about 24 hours.

When you are ready to cook, crush the chillies and garlic together with a pinch of salt using a pestle and mortar (or a blender), to make a fine masala paste.

Heat 150ml of the oil in a large lidded frying pan for about 1 minute over a high heat, then add the okra chunks and fry for about 6 minutes, stirring occasionally. They will sizzle and spit, as this process part-cooks them and removes any remaining moisture, which in turn helps them to absorb the spices and other flavours. Remove the okra from the frying pan a spoonful at a time, squeezing it against the side of the pan to drain off any excess oil, and put it back on the baking tray.

Add the remaining 25ml of oil to the pan containing the okra-infused oil. Heat over a medium heat for 30 seconds, then add the fenugreek and mustard seeds.

When the mustard seeds start to pop, stir in the asafetida and tomatoes. Reduce the heat to low and stir in the masala paste, salt, turmeric, ground coriander, ground cumin and half the fresh coriander. Cook uncovered for about 3 minutes, stirring occasionally, while the herbs and spices infuse the sauce.

Return the okra to the pan and gently stir into the sauce, taking care not to break the delicate pieces, as they add to the texture and structure of the dish. Cover and simmer for about 4 minutes over a medium heat, then remove from the heat and leave to rest, covered, for at least 10 minutes to allow the flavours to infuse.

Reheat over a low heat, sprinkle with the remaining chopped coriander, and serve with *khudi* (page 193) and *baath* (page 156).

Mushroom palak –
Spinach and mushroom curry

(V, WF, N, HO)

As part of my daughter-in-law Minal's training at Gordon Ramsay's restaurants, she worked at Petrus, to see how Michelin-starred restaurants are run. Among other things, she was really impressed by their use of locally sourced ingredients. We already use local spinach and mushrooms for this dish, and hopefully soon we'll be using home-grown ingredients from Minal's new vegetable garden! I cut the spinach into strips the day before cooking this dish, because it helps to dry out some of the moisture in the leaves in advance of cooking, but you can use the spinach fresh if you prefer.

SERVES 4

1kg fresh leaf spinach

150ml sunflower oil

1 teaspoon fenugreek seeds

1 teaspoon brown mustard seeds

¼ teaspoon asafetida

370g button mushrooms,
  cleaned and halved

2 medium tomatoes, roughly chopped

1¼ teaspoons salt

1½ teaspoons turmeric

2–4 teaspoons ground coriander

½ teaspoon ground cumin

1 teaspoon *garam masala*

1 handful of fresh coriander,
  finely chopped

Masala

3–6 fresh green chillies, seeds left in

3–6 cloves of garlic

5cm root ginger, peeled and
  roughly chopped

pinch of salt

Rinse and trim the spinach, then cut into 1cm-wide strips. Leave uncovered at room temperature overnight to dry.

When you're ready to cook, crush the chillies, garlic and ginger together with a pinch of salt using a pestle and mortar (or a blender), to make a fine masala paste.

Heat the oil in a large pan for 1 minute over a medium heat, then add the fenugreek seeds and mustard seeds. When the mustard seeds start to pop, stir in the asafetida and mushrooms. Cook uncovered for 2 minutes or so, gently stirring, then mix in the masala paste, tomatoes, salt, turmeric, ground coriander, ground cumin, *garam masala* and chopped coriander.

Stir over a medium heat for a couple of minutes, then add the spinach. The chopped leaves will be bulky, so you may need to do this in several stages – add as much as you can, cover the pan and allow it to wilt down for a couple of minutes before stirring in, then add the next batch. Repeat the process until all the spinach has been incorporated. Increase the heat to high and cook uncovered for 6 minutes or so, until the water released by the spinach and mushrooms has evaporated.

Remove from the heat and leave to rest, uncovered, for at least 10 minutes to allow the flavours to infuse.

Gently reheat over a low heat and, once hot through again, serve with *paratha* (page 174), *mung dhal kichdi* (page 167) and *khudi* (page 193).

Ratalu –
Garlicky curried purple yam

(V, WF, N, HO)

Whenever you hear of an unusual Gujarati dish, you can be pretty sure my husband likes it. He is a true Gujarati gentleman who loves 'old school' traditional food. Happily I love to cook it for him, and I am particularly fond of purple yams, both for their sweetness and their gorgeous lavender colour. These yams have a thick uneven skin, and you need to peel off quite a lot of it to reach the slightly sticky, sweet lilac flesh inside. This dish is a Sunday feast treat.

SERVES 4

150ml sunflower oil
1½ teaspoons brown mustard seeds
¼ teaspoon asafetida
1 kg purple yams, peeled and cut
 into 1.5cm cubes
1 medium onion, cut into 1cm cubes
1¼ teaspoons salt
1½ teaspoons sugar
1½ teaspoons turmeric
1 tablespoon ground coriander
½ teaspoon ground cumin
2 handfuls of fresh coriander,
 finely chopped

Masala
4–6 fresh green chillies, seeds left in
2–4 cloves of garlic
3cm root ginger, peeled and
 roughly chopped
pinch of salt

Crush the chillies, garlic and ginger together with a pinch of salt using a pestle and mortar (or a blender), to make a fine masala paste.

Heat the oil in a large pan for 1 minute over a medium heat, then add the mustard seeds. When they start to pop, stir in the asafetida, purple yams and onion. Mix well and reduce the heat to low. Add the masala paste, salt, sugar, turmeric, ground coriander, ground cumin and half the fresh coriander, mix thoroughly to combine, then stir in 50ml of boiling water.

Bring to a gentle simmer, then cover and cook over a low heat for 15 minutes or so, stirring regularly, until all the water has evaporated. Check to see whether the yam is cooked – a knife tip should slide in easily. If it needs a little longer, add another 50ml of boiling water, cover the pan again and leave to cook for another 5 minutes, stirring every so often, until cooked through.

As this is a relatively dry dish, it does not need to be rested before serving. Sprinkle with the remaining chopped coriander and serve immediately, with *dhal* (page 192), *baath* (page 156) and *mura raitu* (page 212).

Kehra na reveya –
Green banana satay

(V, WF, HO)

*My husband's grandfather, Lallu Dada, was famous in his village for two things –
his amazing-tasting* reveyas *and his big wobbly belly. Some of his genes have been generously
shared with his grandson Mohan and our son Bobby . . . The green unripe bananas in this dish give
it a starchy sweetness that contrasts really nicely with the spicy peanut sauce. Please note that
you don't peel the bananas before cooking, as the skins serve to hold them together around
the satay filling – Mohan eats the cooked skins, but I prefer not to.*

SERVES 4

100g red-skinned (unroasted,
  unsalted) peanuts, finely chopped
  or blended
2 teaspoons chickpea flour, sieved
1¼ teaspoons salt
1 teaspoon sugar
2–4 teaspoons ground coriander
½ teaspoon ground cumin
1 handful of fresh coriander,
  finely chopped
1 teaspoon turmeric
1 teaspoon cumin seeds
100ml sunflower oil
4 green unripe bananas in their skins,
  rinsed and dried

Masala

3–5 fresh green chillies, seeds left in
3–6 cloves of garlic
4cm root ginger, peeled and
  roughly chopped
pinch of salt

Crush the chillies, garlic and ginger together with a pinch
of salt using a pestle and mortar (or a blender), to make a
fine masala paste.

Put the chopped peanuts and chickpea flour into a medium
bowl and mix together well, using your fingertips. Add the
masala paste, salt, sugar, ground coriander, ground cumin,
fresh coriander, turmeric, cumin seeds and oil and mix them
into the flour and peanuts, still using your hands. Work
everything into a lovely rich paste, then leave to rest for
15 minutes while the spices infuse.

Do not peel the bananas! Chop them into thirds, then cut
each piece lengthways in quarters, leaving the last centimetre
or so at one end intact to hold them together. Gently open
the banana pieces and spread the cut surfaces with the spicy
peanut paste. Place the pieces in a large lidded pan or frying
pan. Scoop any leftover paste into the pan and dot between
the banana pieces.

Place the pan over a high heat and cook for a minute. Pour
300ml of warm water into the paste bowl and swirl it around
to loosen the last of it, then pour this diluted mixture into the
pan, taking care to pour it in between the bananas so as not to
wash the paste out of the incisions. Reduce the heat to medium, cover and leave to cook for 1 minute.

Reduce the heat to very low and leave to cook slowly for 13–15 minutes, carefully turning the banana
pieces every 3–5 minutes to ensure that they are completely infused with the spicy sauce.

There is no need to rest this dish, as the flavours have had time to develop during the slow cooking
process. Serve it immediately, with *paratha* (page 174) and *kacha* tomato relish (page 207). It does
not reheat well (the bananas tend to fall apart), so you have a great excuse to eat it all up in one go!

Mattar paneer –
Sweet and spicy cheese and peas

(WF, OG, N)

This is a traditional Punjabi dish with a fantastic combination of sweet, fresh and spicy flavours. I was inspired to create my version after eating mattar paneer *in a lovely restaurant we went to when we were travelling through Rajasthan. The* paneer *was cooked to perfection – crisp on the outside, meltingly soft in the middle. Bliss. I use frozen* petits pois *for this dish, as they tend to be sweeter and more tender than garden peas.*

SERVES 4

7cm root ginger, peeled and
   roughly chopped
200g frozen peas (ideally *petits pois*)
sunflower oil, for frying, plus 100ml
380g *paneer* cheese, cut into
   1.5cm cubes
1 teaspoon cumin seeds
1 x 400g tin of peeled plum
   tomatoes, finely chopped
   or blended
2 teaspoons medium
   red chilli powder
2 teaspoons turmeric
2–4 teaspoons ground coriander
½ teaspoon ground cumin
1¼ teaspoons salt
1 handful of fresh coriander,
   finely chopped

Crush the ginger with a pestle and mortar (or in a blender) to make a fine pulp. Rinse the peas in warm water to start them thawing.

Heat the frying oil – about 15cm deep – in a large pan over a high heat (or in a deep fat fryer, if you have one). Test the temperature by dropping a piece of *paneer* into the oil – when it is hot enough, the oil will bubble around the cheese. Reduce the heat to medium.

Gently lower the *paneer* cubes into the oil and fry for 1½–2 minutes, until they start to turn golden brown. Be particularly careful while they fry, as the moisture in the cheese can sizzle and spit when it meets the hot oil. Remove from the oil with a slotted spoon and leave to rest on kitchen paper to drain.

Heat 100ml of oil in a separate large pan for 90 seconds over a medium heat, then add the cumin seeds. When they start to brown, reduce the heat to low and stir in the tomatoes. Add the ginger pulp, chilli powder, turmeric, ground coriander, ground cumin, salt and fresh coriander. Mix well and allow to cook for a minute, then stir in the *paneer* cubes and peas. Increase the heat to high and pour in 275ml of boiling water. Bring to the boil, then reduce the heat to medium and simmer three-quarters covered for 8–10 minutes, stirring occasionally.

Remove from the heat and leave to rest, covered, for at least 10 minutes to allow the flavours to develop.

Spoon off any excess oil released by the *paneer* during cooking, then reheat over a medium heat until piping hot and serve with *bathura* (page 178) or *puri* (page 177) and *masala kakadhi* (page 199).

Paneer masala –
Spicy tomato and Indian cheese

(WF, N)

My wonderful daughter-in-law Minal learned how to make this dish while attending professional cooking courses in India. It's one of our most popular main courses and one of my favourite dishes – the buttery, spicy tomato sauce and firm-textured fried paneer *make a great partnership.*

SERVES 4

6cm root ginger, peeled and
  roughly chopped
2–4 fresh green chillies, seeds left in
4–6 cloves of garlic
sunflower oil, for frying, plus 75ml
500g *paneer* cheese, cut into
  1.5cm cubes
1 medium onion, finely chopped
  or blended to a smooth paste
1 x 400g tin of peeled plum
  tomatoes, finely chopped or blended
1¼ teaspoons salt
1½ teaspoons turmeric
2–4 teaspoons ground coriander
½ teaspoon ground cumin
2 handfuls of fresh coriander,
  finely chopped
50g unsalted butter
½ teaspoon *garam masala*

Crush the ginger using a pestle and mortar (or a blender), to make a fine pulp. Cut the chillies into fine rings and chop the garlic finely.

Heat the frying oil – about 15cm deep – in a large pan over a high heat (or in a deep fat fryer, if you have one). Test the temperature by dropping a piece of *paneer* into the oil – when it is hot enough, the oil will bubble around the cheese. Reduce the heat to medium.

Gently lower the *paneer* cubes into the oil and fry for 1½–2 minutes, until they start to turn golden brown. Be particularly careful while they fry, as the moisture in the cheese can sizzle and spit when it meets the hot oil. Remove the fried cubes from the oil with a slotted spoon and leave to rest on kitchen paper to drain.

Heat 75ml of oil in a separate large pan for 90 seconds over a medium heat, then add the chillies and garlic and fry for 20 seconds, stirring constantly. Increase the heat to high, add the onion and fry until it is dark brown. I do this by covering the pan and leaving the onion to cook for 2 minutes before stirring, then covering again and repeating 3 or 4 times until it has caramelized to a lovely dark brown, taking care not to burn it.

Reduce the heat to low and stir in the tomatoes. Add the ginger pulp, salt, turmeric, ground coriander, ground cumin and half the fresh coriander and mix through. Return the heat to high and simmer uncovered for a minute, then stir in the *paneer* and butter. Pour in 100ml of boiling water and bring the mixture to the boil. Cover and simmer over a low heat for 8 minutes.

Stir in the *garam masala* and the remaining coriander, then remove from the heat and leave to rest, covered, for at least 15 minutes to allow the flavours to infuse.

Reheat over a medium heat until steaming hot, then serve with *rotli* (page 170) or *puri* (page 177), *pilau baath* (page 157) and either *kandha raitu* (page 212) or *phudino dai* (page 211).

Tarka dhal –
Curried red and yellow lentils
(V, WF, N, HO)

In Gujarat, you find many makeshift streetside cafés serving great-tasting food. One of the most popular dishes is tarka dhal, *or* dhal *fry, which is the staple meal for drivers when they're on the road – rather different from the traditional British greasy fry-up. When my son Bobby is seriously trying to lose weight, his evening meal will always be* tarka dhal *and mixed salad. The* tarka *is the spiced oil used to season the* dhal *– tempering the spices in hot oil in this way helps to maximize the flavours.*

SERVES 4

150g *masoor dhal* (split red lentils)

150g *mung dhal* (yellow split mung beans)

1 teaspoon sunflower oil, plus 100ml for the *tarka* (spiced oil)

1 teaspoon cumin seeds

½ teaspoon brown mustard seeds

¼ teaspoon asafetida

3 medium tomatoes, roughly chopped or blended

1 teaspoon turmeric

1½ teaspoons salt

2–4 teaspoons ground coriander

½ teaspoon ground cumin

½ teaspoon *garam masala*

1 handful of fresh coriander, finely chopped

Masala

3–5 fresh green chillies, seeds left in

3–5 cloves of garlic

pinch of salt

Mix the *dhals* together, then rinse at least 4 times in warm water (see page 25) and drain.

Crush the chillies and garlic together with a pinch of salt using a pestle and mortar (or in a blender) to make a fine masala paste.

Put the *dhals* into a large pan and add 700ml of boiling water. Bring to the boil, then simmer over a medium heat for a couple of minutes until it starts to foam. Skim the froth from the surface, add the teaspoon of oil and simmer three-quarters covered for 25 minutes or so, stirring occasionally, until the *dhals* are soft and cooked through. Remove the pan from the heat and set aside, but do not drain.

Heat the oil in a separate large pan for 30 seconds over a medium heat, then add the cumin and mustard seeds. When the mustard seeds start to pop, stir in the asafetida, then reduce the heat to low and add the tomatoes – be careful, as the water in them may make them spit when they touch the oil.

Stir in the masala paste, turmeric, salt, ground coriander and ground cumin. Increase the heat to medium and leave to cook for a minute, then stir in the *dhals*, along with the water in which they were cooked. Pour in 100ml of boiling water, stir, simmer for 2 minutes, then stir in the *garam masala*. Adding the *garam masala* right at the end ensures that it is the first spice you taste, with the other spices following on for a deeper, longer-lasting flavour.

Remove from the heat, sprinkle with the fresh coriander, then cover the pan and leave to rest for at least 10 minutes to allow the flavours to infuse.

Reheat over a medium heat and serve piping hot, with *puri* (page 177) and *masala kakadhi* (page 199) – or, if you are dieting like Bobby, just a mixed salad.

Vegetable handi ~
Tomato and chunky vegetable curry

(V, WF, N, HO)

A handi is a round, deep, thick-bottomed cooking pot, which is covered and placed directly on charcoals to cook dishes that need lengthy simmering to bring out their full flavour. When my husband and I first opened Prashad, we used to sell our food at Indian outdoor festivals like Bradford Mela. *Aromatic, delicious and deeply satisfying, this was one of our best-sellers.*

SERVES 4

100ml sunflower oil

1 teaspoon cumin seeds

1 medium onion, finely chopped
  or blended to a fine paste

1 x 400g tin of peeled plum tomatoes,
  finely chopped or blended

1 small red-skinned (or other waxy)
  potato, cut into 1.5cm cubes

1 medium carrot, cut into 5mm discs

1½ teaspoons salt

1½ teaspoons turmeric

2–4 teaspoons ground coriander

½ teaspoon ground cumin

1 handful of fresh coriander,
  finely chopped

1 small red pepper, deseeded and
  cut into 1.5cm cubes

1 small green pepper, deseeded and
  cut into 1.5cm cubes

1 small cauliflower,
  cut into small florets

150g fresh or frozen peas

½ teaspoon *garam masala*

Masala

2–4 fresh green chillies, seeds left in

1–3 cloves of garlic

5cm root ginger, peeled and
  roughly chopped

pinch of salt

Crush the chillies, garlic and ginger together with a pinch of salt using a pestle and mortar (or a blender), to make a fine masala paste.

Heat the oil in a large pan for 90 seconds over a medium heat, then add the cumin seeds. When they start to brown, stir in the onion – be careful, as the moisture in it may spit when it meets the hot oil. Increase the heat to high, cover the pan and leave it to cook for a minute before stirring, then cover again and repeat 3 or 4 times until the onion has caramelized to a lovely dark brown (take care not to burn it). This browning of the onion is important, as it gives the dish its rich colour and sweet flavour.

Stir in the tomatoes, potato, carrot and 300ml of boiling water. Cover and leave to simmer for 7–8 minutes over a high heat. Add the masala paste, salt, turmeric, ground coriander, ground cumin and fresh coriander and mix well. Stir in the peppers, cauliflower and another 100ml of boiling water, being careful not to break up the vegetables.

Reduce the heat to medium, then cover the pan and simmer for 10 minutes. Stir in the peas along with a final 50ml of boiling water, then cover again and simmer for a further 5 minutes. Check to see whether the potato is cooked through – if not, reduce the heat to low and simmer, covered, for an additional 5 minutes or so until it is done.

Stir in the *garam masala*, remove from the heat, cover and leave to rest for at least 15 minutes to let the flavours develop.

Reheat over a medium heat until piping hot, and serve with *jeera baath* (page 158) and *phudino kandha* (page 211).

Masala dosa –
Crispy pancake with potato and coconut curry

(V, WF, N, HO)

The trick with this dish is getting the pancake right. When we first started selling our food at outdoor festivals, my husband would watch from afar to see how other traders made their pancakes. He has combined his observations with his own research over the years to create the process for making the very best dosas. *Broken rice (broken or cracked during harvesting or drying) tends to be starchier than whole rice and so makes great sticky rice and porridge – it is perfect here because the starch helps to make the* dosas *lovely and crispy. Do note that you will need to start preparing the batter ingredients a couple of days before you want to make* masala dosas, *to allow soaking and fermenting time. This dish tastes best made with fresh coconut, but if you can't get hold of any, use 25g of unsweetened desiccated coconut instead.*

SERVES 4 (MAKES 8)

sunflower oil, for drizzling

Batter
(start at least 32 hours / 2 days before cooking)
275g broken rice
65g *urad dhal* (white lentils)
½ teaspoon fenugreek seeds
1½ teaspoons salt
1 teaspoon granulated sugar

Masala
3–5 fresh green chillies, seeds left in
4cm root ginger, peeled and roughly chopped
pinch of salt

Filling
100ml sunflower oil
1 teaspoon cumin seeds
1 teaspoon brown mustard seeds
¼ teaspoon asafetida
10 fresh curry leaves
2 medium onions, cut into 1cm cubes

Mix the rice, *dhal* and fenugreek seeds together, then rinse 3 times in warm water (see top tips on page 25). Put into a large bowl, pour in enough warm water to cover and leave to soak for 12 hours or overnight.

Drain the soaked rice/*dhal*/seed mixture and grind in 2 batches in a food mixer or blender, adding 100ml of cold water to each batch to help the grinding. I usually leave each batch blending for about 5 minutes. Don't skimp this process, as the more you grind it, the frothier the pulped mixture will become and the crispier the finished *dosa* will be.

Put the mixture into a large bowl and whisk thoroughly, then pour into an airtight container. Refrigerate for 24 hours while the batter ferments – this is what makes the *dosa* pancake so deliciously fluffy.

When you are ready to make the *masala dosa*, crush the chillies and ginger together with a pinch of salt using a pestle and mortar (or in a blender), to make a fine masala paste.

Heat the oil in a large pan for 1 minute over a medium heat, then add the cumin seeds and mustard seeds. When

4 medium red-skinned
  (or other waxy) potatoes,
  cut into 2cm cubes
¼ small fresh coconut, finely
  grated into long strands
1 teaspoon salt
1 teaspoon sugar
pinch of turmeric
1 teaspoon *garam masala*
1 handful of fresh coriander,
  finely chopped

the mustard seeds start to pop, add the asafetida and reduce the heat to low. Stir in the curry leaves, followed by the onions and potatoes. Cook for a minute, uncovered, stirring to coat the vegetables in the oil, then stir in the masala paste and all the other filling ingredients.

Increase the heat to high and cook for 3–4 minutes, stirring regularly. Reduce the heat to low, cover the pan and cook for 10 minutes or so, until the potato is cooked through, still stirring regularly to make sure nothing is sticking or scorching. Remove from the heat and set aside.

Whisk the salt and sugar into the fermented batter and check the texture – it should be pourable. If it seems stiff, stir in 100ml of cold water and whisk again. Heat a non-stick frying pan over a low heat until a little water sprinkled on it immediately sizzles and bubbles away. Pour about 150ml of batter into the middle of the pan, then use a heatproof spatula, a palette knife or the back of a ladle to spread it over the surface of the pan, starting in the middle and working outwards in a circular motion.

Increase the heat to medium and drizzle a little oil around the edges. Fry the pancake for 1–2 minutes, until the edges start to lift away from the pan. Then spoon an eighth of the filling into the centre of the pancake. Fold the edges over so that you have a filled pancake roll. Turn it over and cook the other side for a minute, then lift out and place on a large plate.

Repeat this process until you have 4 filled *dosas*. Serve each one with a bowl of hot *sambar* (page 190) and a good spoonful or two of *kopru* dip (page 214) on the side. Sit down and enjoy eating the first round of *dosas* before making the second, so that they are hot and fresh each time. Any additional batter can be fried to make more plain pancakes, which also taste great with the *sambar* and *kopru*.

RICE AND BREADS

RICE AND BREADS

Whatever the occasion, there are two things you will always find at any traditional Gujarati meal: rice and bread. As a result, we try to keep our rice as light and fluffy as possible and our *rotli* very thin and delicate, in order to maintain some control over the amount of carbohydrate we're eating!

Rice is part of the staple diet throughout India, especially if you come from rice-farming families, as Mohan and I do. I use long-grained basmati rice, as it has a wonderful delicate flavour and is less starchy than short-grained rice. It takes centre stage in simple dishes like *baath* steamed rice, *lila dhania baath* green coriander rice and fresh pea *wattana pilau*, but is also wonderful playing more of a supporting role in stronger-flavoured dishes like cumin-infused *jeera baath* and spicy vegetable *pilau baath*.

Aromatic basmati combines beautifully with *dhal* to create *mung* and *tuvar dhal kichdi* – warming, filling comfort food, perfect for when you're feeling tired or run-down. And it comes into its own in one-pot meals like mouth-watering vegetable, rice and lentil *biryani* and my own creation, *batsai kichdi*, with its delicious layers of spiced rice and *dhal*, aubergine, yoghurt and fried vegetables.

The main bread in Gujarati cuisine is *rotli*, a soft thin chapatti bread which is torn in bite-sized pieces and used instead of a fork to pick up food. *Bhakri* is a slightly thicker, rustic version made with *ghee* instead of oil, while *rotla* is a fat-free bread made with gluten-free sorghum flour, making it a good option for people with dietary restrictions.

There are richer fried breads – try flaky *paratha*, moreish deep-fried *puri* puffs and soft chewy *bathura* – and indulgent sweetened breads too, like seed-topped golden *mal pura* and rich butter-drenched *velmi*, stuffed with sweet cardamom *dhal*. Each can be eaten either on its own as a tempting snack or as a great accompaniment to a full meal.

There's such variety in the taste, texture and appearance of the different Indian breads, and everyone in my home has their favourite: I really enjoy *velmi*, Mohan is a *bhakri* fan, Bobby adores *bathura*, Minal prefers *rotli* and Mayur loves *paratha*. Why not try your hand at some of these recipes and find out which is your favourite?

RICE AND BREADS

Lila dhania baath – Green coriander rice

(V, WF, N, HO)

I first came across this dish in a competition. The other finalist was cooking an amazing green rice dish with a mouth-watering aroma, and even though I eventually won the competition, I knew that when I got home I would have to cook my own version of that flavoursome green rice for my husband. The fragrant basmati and fresh coriander are just wonderful together.

SERVES 4

350g basmati rice
50ml sunflower oil
1 teaspoon cumin seeds
1¼ teaspoons salt

Masala

2–3 fresh green chillies,
  seeds left in
1–2 cloves of garlic
3 handfuls of fresh coriander,
  finely chopped
pinch of salt

Crush the chillies, garlic and coriander together with a pinch of salt using a pestle and mortar (or a blender), to make a fine masala paste.

Rinse the rice twice in warm water, then drain. Heat the oil in a large pan for a minute over a medium heat, then add the cumin seeds. Keep an eye on them, and when they start to go brown, tip in the rice, masala paste and salt, pour in 1 litre of boiling water and stir gently.

Increase the heat to high and boil uncovered for 7–8 minutes, stirring occasionally, until almost all the water has evaporated and the rice starts to look dry. Put a large square of foil on top, tucking it round the rice to keep it moist and fluffy while it steams. Put a lid on the pan, then reduce the heat to the lowest setting and leave to cook for 8–9 minutes. Remove from the heat and leave to rest, covered, for at least 5 minutes.

When you remove the foil, the rice should be perfectly cooked. Gently run a spoon through it to loosen the grains, and serve straight away with plain live set yoghurt and *masala kakadhi* (page 199).

Baath –
Boiled basmati rice

(V, WF, OG, N, HO)

Back in India, our families are farmers whose main crop is rice. This isn't surprising, given that the main part of any Gujarati meal will always be accompanied by a serving of rice. Basmati rice, with its long grains and delicate flavour, tends to be less starchy than shorter-grained rice. It also has a sweet fragrance that gives rise to its name – 'basmati' means 'full of aroma' in Hindi. I always use Tilda basmati rice because I find that it has the best flavour.

SERVES 4

300g basmati rice
40ml sunflower oil
½ teaspoon salt

Rinse the rice twice in warm water, then drain. Heat the oil in a large pan over a medium heat for 30 seconds. Add the rice and stir gently, then add the salt and 900ml of boiling water.

Boil the rice uncovered over a high heat for 10 minutes or so, stirring occasionally, until almost all the water has evaporated and the rice starts to look dry. Put a large square of foil on top, tucking it round the sides, then put a lid on the pan, reduce the heat to the lowest setting and leave to cook for 7–8 minutes. Remove from the heat and set aside to rest, covered, for at least 5 minutes.

When you remove the foil, the rice should be perfectly cooked. Gently run a spoon through it to loosen the grains, and serve straight away. I love to eat *baath* with *dhal* (page 192) or *khudi* (page 193), but it goes with most dishes, so take your pick!

Pilau baath –
Spiced vegetable rice

(V, WF, N, HO)

Pilau rice, also called pulao *or* pilaf, *is originally a Persian dish, but variations on it can be found all across the world. Pilau is practically a meal in itself – a great combination of rice, vegetables and spices – and sometimes I just eat it with yoghurt as a light lunch or supper. It is my daughter Hina's favourite rice dish, and the first thing she thinks of when she is planning to cook Indian food.*

SERVES 4

50g fresh or frozen peas
  (ideally *petits pois*)
300g basmati rice
75m sunflower oil
1 teaspoon cumin seeds
½ small green pepper, deseeded
  and cut into small (5mm) cubes
½ small red pepper, deseeded
  and cut into small (5mm) cubes
1 small red-skinned (or other waxy)
  potato, peeled and cut into
  small (5mm) cubes
1¼ teaspoons salt
¼ teaspoon turmeric

Masala
2–6 fresh green chillies, seeds left in
2–4 cloves of garlic
3cm root ginger, peeled and
  roughly chopped
pinch of salt

Crush the chillies, garlic and ginger together with a pinch of salt using a pestle and mortar (or a blender), to make a fine masala paste. If using frozen peas, rinse them in warm water to start them thawing.

Rinse the rice twice in warm water, then drain. Heat the oil in a large pan for a minute over a medium heat, then stir in the cumin seeds. Keep an eye on them, and when they start to go brown, add the rice, peas, peppers and potato and stir gently. Reduce the heat to low, add the salt, turmeric and masala paste, then pour in 900ml of boiling water and gently stir everything together.

Increase the heat to high and boil uncovered for 8–10 minutes, stirring occasionally, until almost all the water has evaporated and the rice starts to look dry. Put a large square of foil on top, tucking it round the sides, then put a lid on the pan, reduce the heat to the lowest setting and leave to cook for 7–8 minutes. Remove from the heat and leave to rest, covered, for at least 5 minutes.

When you remove the foil, everything should be perfectly cooked. Gently run a spoon through it to loosen the grains, and serve straight away as a delicious accompaniment to any curry – or, if *pilau baath* is the main part of your meal, with plain live set yoghurt or a bowl of *khudi* (page 193).

Jeera baath –
Cumin-infused rice

(V, WF, N, HO)

Jeera baath is a firm favourite at the restaurant. Infusing the onion with cumin gives this rice a bold flavour, so we serve it with other strongly flavoured dishes, particularly spicy tomato-based Punjabi ones. Its perfect partner is chole (page 132).

SERVES 4

300g basmati rice
75ml sunflower oil
1 teaspoon cumin seeds
1 medium onion,
  chopped in rings
1¼ teaspoons salt

Rinse the rice twice in warm water, then drain. Heat the oil in a large pan for 1 minute over a medium heat, then stir in the cumin seeds. Keep an eye on them as they bubble in the oil, and when they start to go brown, stir in the onion.

Increase the heat to high, cover the pan and leave the onion to cook gently for 2 minutes before stirring. Repeat this covered cooking and stirring several times, until the onion has caramelized to a lovely dark brown (this should take about 7–8 minutes). The browning of the onion is important, as the more time you take at this stage to infuse it in the cumin oil, the richer the flavour and the deeper the colour of the finished dish.

Add the rice, stir gently, then add the salt and 900ml of boiling water and stir gently again. Boil uncovered for 6–7 minutes, stirring occasionally, until almost all the water has evaporated and the rice starts to look dry. Put a large square of foil on top, tucking it round the sides, then put a lid on the pan, reduce the heat to the lowest setting and leave to cook for 6–7 minutes. Remove from the heat and set aside to rest, covered, for at least 5 minutes.

When you remove the foil, everything should be perfectly cooked. Gently run a spoon through it to loosen the grains, and serve straight away with *chole* (page 132) and *phudino dai* (page 211).

Batsai kichdi –
The king of rice dishes

(WF, N)

This dish is my own creation and one of which I am very proud. It combines spicy rice and dhal, aubergine curry, creamy yoghurt, fried peppers and crunchy onions to become the royalty of rice dishes and a full meal in itself. I have passed this recipe on to my children, and now I am sharing it with you. Every ingredient plays its part, and when they all come together in the alternating layers of different flavours, colours and textures they make something truly wonderful.

SERVES 6

Masala 1

2–4 fresh green chillies, seeds left in
2–4 cloves of garlic
3cm root ginger, peeled and
  roughly chopped
pinch of salt

Masala 2

2–4 fresh green chillies, seeds left in
5cm root ginger, peeled and
  roughly chopped
pinch of salt

Dhal and rice

200g *tuvar dhal* (dried pigeon peas/
  yellow lentils)
200g basmati rice
50ml sunflower oil
1 teaspoon salt
¼ teaspoon turmeric

Fried vegetables

sunflower oil, for frying
1 small green pepper, deseeded and
  cut into 2cm cubes
1 small red pepper, deseeded and
  cut into 2cm cubes
2 medium onions, cut into
  5mm-wide rings

(continued on page 162)

Crush the ingredients for each masala separately, using a pestle and mortar (or a blender), to make a fine paste.

Rinse the *tuvar dhal* at least 3 times in hot water (see page 25), then leave to soak in hot water for at least 10 minutes before draining. Rinse the rice twice in warm water, then drain.

Heat the 50ml of oil for the *dhal* in a large pan for 1 minute over a medium heat. Add the *dhal* and rice and fry together for 1 minute, gently stirring to coat them in oil. Add the salt, turmeric and the first masala paste, stir, then pour in 800ml of boiling water. Increase the heat to high and cook for 1 minute, uncovered, to bring to the boil, then reduce the heat to medium and simmer half-covered for 8–10 minutes, stirring occasionally, until most of the water has evaporated.

Put a large square of foil on top, tucking it round the sides, then put a lid on the pan, reduce the heat to the lowest setting and leave to cook for 8–10 minutes. Remove from the heat and leave to rest, covered, for at least 5 minutes, then remove the lid and foil and leave the rice and *dhal* to cool in the pan.

Heat the oil for the vegetables in a frying pan over a high heat. Fry the pepper chunks for 3 minutes or so, then remove from the pan and leave to rest on kitchen paper. Fry the onion rings in a couple of batches until they are dark brown (this should take about 4–5 minutes) and leave to rest on kitchen paper. Don't be tempted to rush the frying, as the crunchy onions add an important texture to the dish.

Heat the 100ml of oil for the curry in a large pan for 1 minute over a medium heat, then add the cumin and mustard seeds. When the mustard seeds start to pop, add the asafetida along with the aubergines and potatoes. Stir and reduce the heat to low. Stir in the second masala paste, turmeric, salt, ground coriander, ground cumin and 50ml of warm water. Bring to the boil, then cover

Aubergine curry

100ml sunflower oil
1 teaspoon cumin seeds
1 teaspoon brown mustard seeds
¼ teaspoon asafetida
2 medium aubergines,
  cut into 3cm cubes
2 medium red-skinned (or other
  waxy) potatoes,
  cut into 2cm cubes
1 teaspoon turmeric
1¼ teaspoons salt
2 teaspoons ground coriander
½ teaspoon ground cumin
2 medium tomatoes, roughly chopped
1 handful of fresh coriander,
  finely chopped
90g unsalted butter
500g plain live set yoghurt

and cook over a low heat for 7–8 minutes. Stir in the tomatoes and chopped coriander, simmer for a further 5 minutes or so, until the potatoes are cooked through, then remove from the heat.

Tip the cooled rice and *dhal* into a large roasting dish or baking tray. Spread it out, then stir in the butter. Whisk the yoghurt for a couple of minutes until slightly runny.

Spoon about a third of the rice back into the cooking pan to form a layer roughly 2cm thick (depending on the size of your pan). Follow with half the aubergine curry, then half the whisked yoghurt. Sprinkle the yoghurt with a third of the fried peppers and onions. Repeat the layering, starting with half the remaining rice, followed by the rest of the aubergine curry, then the rest of the yoghurt topped with half the remaining fried vegetables. Use the rest of the rice to create the final layer, and sprinkle the remaining peppers and onions over the top.

Put a large square of foil on top, tucking it round the sides, then put a lid on the pan and place it over a high heat for a minute. Reduce the heat to the lowest setting and leave to cook for 25 minutes or so, then remove from the heat and leave to rest, covered, for at least 10 minutes.

Serve piping hot, spooning up from the bottom of the pan to make sure each serving contains all the different layers. Enjoy it with a glass of chilled mango *lassi* (page 222).

Biryani –
Layered vegetables, rice and lentils

(WF, N)

Biryani is a Prashad family Christmas special. The name comes from the Persian and means fried or roasted. The fried vegetables, rice and dhal are cooked separately, then layered together to form a dish of contrasting flavours and textures. Whole masoor dhal, *used in this dish, has a speckled greenish-brown skin and a reddish-orange centre. The whole lentils have a chewier texture and a stronger flavour than when in red split lentil form, and also take longer to cook, so I precook them separately from the rice.*

SERVES 6–8

½ teaspoon *garam masala*
¾ teaspoon salt
10 dried Indian bay leaves
70g unsalted butter

Dhal
200g whole *masoor dhal*
  (whole red lentils)
1 teaspoon sunflower oil

Fried vegetables
sunflower oil, for frying
2 medium red-skinned
  (or other waxy) potatoes,
  cut into 2cm cubes
2 medium carrots, cut into
  2cm cubes
1 small red pepper, deseeded
  and cut into 3cm cubes
1 small green pepper, deseeded
  and cut into 3cm cubes
1 small yellow pepper, deseeded
  and cut into 3cm cubes
2 medium onions, cut into
  1cm strips

(continued on page 164)

Rinse the *masoor dhal* at least 3 times in warm water (see page 25), then drain and place in a large pan with 650ml of boiling water. Bring to the boil, then simmer over a medium heat for a couple of minutes until it starts to foam. Skim the froth from the surface, add the teaspoon of oil and simmer three-quarters covered for 18–20 minutes, stirring occasionally, until the *dhal* is soft and cooked through. Remove from the heat, drain and set aside.

Heat the frying oil – about 20cm deep – in a large pan (or deep fat fryer, if you have one). Test the temperature by dropping a potato cube into the oil – when it is hot enough, the potato will immediately start to sizzle and bubble. Reduce to the heat to medium.

Carefully lower the potatoes into the oil and use a wooden spoon to move them around so that they cook evenly all over. Fry for 4–5 minutes, or until golden brown and just becoming crisp. Remove from the oil with a slotted spoon and leave to rest on kitchen paper while you fry the other vegetables.

Fry the carrots for 2 minutes, moving them around so that they cook evenly, then remove and leave to rest on kitchen paper. Next fry the pepper pieces for 2–3 minutes, then remove and leave to rest with the potatoes and carrots. Finally, fry the onions for 7–8 minutes and add to the other fried vegetables.

Masala

4–6 fresh green chillies, seeds left in
2–4 cloves of garlic
5cm root ginger, peeled and
  roughly chopped
pinch of salt

Rice

200g basmati rice
100ml sunflower oil
¾ teaspoon salt

Crush the chillies, garlic and ginger together with a pinch of salt using a pestle and mortar (or a blender), to make a fine masala paste.

Rinse the rice twice in warm water, then drain. Heat the 100ml of oil for the rice in a large pan over a high heat for 30 seconds. Add the rice, salt and masala paste and stir gently. Fry together for a minute, then pour in 650ml of boiling water.

Boil the rice uncovered over a high heat for 10–11 minutes, until almost all the water has evaporated and it starts to look dry. Put a large square of foil on top, tucking it round the sides, then put a lid on the pan, reduce the heat to the lowest setting and leave to cook for 5 minutes. Remove from the heat and set aside.

Tip the *dhal* into a large bowl. Add the *garam masala*, salt and bay leaves and mix gently. Add the rice and butter and gently mix again to combine.

Spoon about a third of the rice/*dhal* mixture back into the rice cooking pan to form a layer roughly 2cm thick, followed by half the fried vegetables. Add another layer of rice/*dhal* mixture (about half of what's left), followed by the rest of the fried vegetables. Use the remaining rice/*dhal* to create a final layer.

Put a large square of foil on top, tucking it round the sides, then put a lid on the pan and place it over a high heat for 30 seconds. Reduce the heat to the lowest setting and leave to cook for 18–20 minutes or so, then remove from the heat and set aside to rest, covered, for at least 10 minutes.

Serve piping hot, spooning up from the bottom of the pan to make sure each serving contains all the different layers (removing the bay leaves as you come across them). Enjoy it with a glass of chilled mango *lassi* (page 222).

Mung dhal kichdi – Soothing yellow lentil rice

(V, WF, N, HO)

In Gujarati families, it's traditional to cook this for anyone who falls ill – it's warming, filling and easy to digest. Mung beans are more commonly found as beansprouts in the UK; however, in their dried split form they are simple to cook (there's no need to soak them) and provide a great source of protein. Mung dhal kichdi *is true comfort food, delicious and nutritious whether you're ailing, convalescing or in the peak of health.*

SERVES 4

175g *mung dhal*
  (yellow split mung beans)
175g basmati rice
75ml sunflower oil
2–4 cloves of garlic, finely chopped
1¼ teaspoons salt
¼ teaspoon turmeric

Mix the *dhal* and rice together, then rinse twice in warm water (see page 25) and drain.

Heat the oil in a large pan for a minute over a medium heat. Add the *dhal* and rice and fry together for a minute, stirring gently. Stir in the garlic, salt and turmeric and fry for another minute, then pour in 900ml of boiling water.

Bring to the boil, then simmer uncovered over a medium heat for 10–12 minutes, until almost all the water has evaporated and it starts to look dry. Put a large square of foil on top, tucking it round the sides, then put a lid on the pan, reduce the heat to the lowest setting and leave to cook for 7–8 minutes. Remove from the heat and set aside to rest, covered, for at least 5 minutes.

When you remove the foil, everything should be perfectly cooked. Gently run a spoon through it to loosen the grains, and serve straight away with *khudi* (page 193) and *limbu attana* (page 196).

Tuvar dhal kichdi – Pigeon peas and rice

(V (OPTIONAL), WF, N, OG, HO)

Protein-rich tuvar *or* toor dhal *is made from hulled split pigeon peas and is one of the most popular pulses in India, where it has been grown for more than 3,000 years. You can find many different recipes for* tuvar dhal kichdi; *however, I just use butter and turmeric to create a simple but delicious dish. Whenever my husband has been away on business and is travelling home, I can guarantee that he will be thinking about enjoying this when he gets back. I like to use Malawian* tuvar dhal *because of its depth of flavour and ease of cooking.*

SERVES 4

150g *tuvar dhal*
  (dried pigeon peas/yellow lentils)
200g basmati rice
75ml sunflower oil
1¼ teaspoons salt
½ teaspoon turmeric
45g butter (optional)

Rinse the *tuvar dhal* at least 3 times in hot water (see page 25), then leave to soak in hot water for at least 10 minutes before draining. Rinse the rice twice in warm water, then drain.

Heat the oil in a large pan for 1 minute over a medium heat. Add the *dhal* and rice and fry together for a minute, stirring gently. Stir in the salt, turmeric and 925ml of boiling water.

Bring to the boil, then simmer uncovered over a medium heat for 10–12 minutes, until the majority of the water has evaporated and the *dhal*/rice starts to look dry. Then reduce the heat to its lowest setting and stir in the butter (if using). Put a large square of foil on top, tucking it round the sides, then put a lid on the pan, reduce the heat to the lowest setting and leave to cook for 6–7 minutes. Remove from the heat and leave for at least 5 minutes.

Stir through gently with a spoon to loosen any clumps, and serve immediately with *khudi* (page 193) and *keri attana* (page 194).

Wattana pilau –
Fresh peas and rice

(V, WF, N, HO)

I love to make this dish when peas are in season, as they taste so sweet fresh from the pod and have a wonderful firm texture that combines beautifully with the fluffy basmati rice. This dish is Bobby's favourite – he isn't generally a big rice fan (unlike his wife, Minal, who loves all rice dishes), but this is one he just can't refuse.

SERVES 4

300g basmati rice
100g fresh or frozen peas
 (ideally *petits pois*)
75ml sunflower oil
1 teaspoon brown mustard seeds
1¼ teaspoons salt
pinch of turmeric

Masala
1–3 fresh green chillies, seeds left in
1–3 cloves of garlic
3cm root ginger, peeled and
 roughly chopped
pinch of salt

Rinse the rice twice in warm water, then drain.

Crush the chillies, garlic and ginger together with a pinch of salt using a pestle and mortar (or a blender), to make a fine masala paste. If using frozen peas, rinse them in warm water to start them thawing.

Heat the oil in a large pan for 1 minute over a medium heat, then add the mustard seeds. When they start to pop, add the rice and peas and increase the heat to high. Add the salt, turmeric and masala paste, pour in 1 litre of boiling water, and gently stir everything together.

Boil the rice uncovered for 10–11 minutes, until almost all the water has evaporated and the rice starts to look dry. Put a large square of foil on top, tucking it round the sides, then put a lid on the pan, reduce the heat to the lowest setting and leave to cook for 6–7 minutes. Remove from the heat and set aside to rest for at least 5 minutes.

When you remove the foil, the rice should be perfectly cooked. Gently run a spoon through it to loosen the grains, and serve straight away to accompany your main curry or, if you are eating this dish on its own as a light supper, with a glass of chilled mango *lassi* (page 222).

Rotli –
Traditional puffed flatbread

(OG, N, HO)

Rotli is a soft, thin, unleavened chapatti bread, traditionally used instead of a fork to pick up curry, dhal, pickles or anything else you happen to be eating. Rotlis are cooked in two stages – first they are sealed in a medium hot pan or tawa, *then they are puffed up directly over the heat source. I puff them up over a gas flame; however, if you don't have gas, you can cook the* rotli *on a round mesh screen with a handle (the type designed to stop fat spitting when you're frying), heated on an electric hob, or you can put them into the microwave for 10–20 seconds on a low setting.*

SERVES 4 (MAKES 16)

300g chapatti flour,
  plus extra for flouring
  and rolling
50ml sunflower oil
butter, for greasing

Put the flour into a large bowl, add the oil and 300ml of boiling water, and mix with a spoon until the dough starts to come together and has cooled enough to start using your hands. Knead for at least 2–3 minutes. The more you work the dough, the softer and fluffier the *rotlis* will be. The dough will be quite sticky, so gently smooth the surface with lightly oiled hands, wrap in clingfilm and set aside until you are ready to make the *rotli*.

Divide the dough into 16 roughly equal pieces, then form them into balls between your palms and squash to flatten slightly. Put a flat *tawa* pan or a flat-based non-stick frying pan over a very low heat to warm while you roll the first *rotli* (*tawa* are traditionally very thick, so they take a while to heat up).

Dust a dough ball with chapatti flour (not too much or it will burn), then place it on a lightly floured work surface and roll it into a thin circular disc, about 19–20cm in diameter (see method on page 91). If you find that the dough sticks to the work surface, sprinkle a little more flour underneath.

Increase the heat under the pan to medium, shake any excess flour off the *rotli* and place in the pan. After a minute or so it will start to bubble, cooking the outer layer and sealing it. Turn to seal the other side.

Remove the pan from the heat, increase the gas to high and use tongs to lay the *rotli* straight on the gas ring. As soon as it has puffed up, remove from the heat, place on kitchen paper and smear with a little butter to grease the surface and stop the next *rotli* from sticking to it. Repeat the rolling, sealing and puffing process until all the *rotlis* are cooked and stacked on top of each other. If you are making them in advance of serving, wrap them in foil to stop them drying out. Serve while still warm, or allow to cool and reheat in the pan for a minute or two over a medium heat before serving.

Rotlis can be served with pretty much any meal, but they go particularly well with *renghan reveya* (page 108), *renghan bataka* (page 111), *wattana* and flower (page 118), *sukhu bhinda bataka* (page 124), *makai* (page 121) or *paneer masala* (page 142). Any leftover *rotlis* can be stored in an airtight container (once they've cooled) and reheated in the *tawa* or frying pan the next day. Alternatively you can use them to make *vagareli rotli* (page 87) for lunch or a light supper.

Bhakri – Rustic flatbread

(OG, N)

Bhakri is a thicker and more substantial flatbread than rotli, *and the sugar and* ghee *in the dough make it a more luxurious addition to a meal. My husband would eat it every evening, given the choice.*

SERVES 4–6 (MAKES 12)

300g chapatti flour
50ml *ghee* (or clarified butter), melted
2 teaspoons sugar
12 teaspoons oil, for frying

Combine the flour, *ghee* and sugar in a large bowl, using your hands to make sure the *ghee* is thoroughly worked in. Pour in 200ml of warm water and mix until the dough starts to come together. Knead for a couple of minutes until firm and smooth, taking care not to overwork it. Wrap in lightly oiled clingfilm and set aside until you are ready to cook the *bhakri*.

Divide the dough into 12 roughly equal pieces, then form them into balls between your palms and squash to flatten slightly. Place a flattened dough ball on a clean work surface and roll it into a disc about 12cm in diameter and roughly 5mm thick (see method on page 91). Repeat with the remaining dough balls, placing the discs on a baking sheet as you go, making sure they don't overlap.

Heat a flat *tawa* pan or a flat-based non-stick frying pan over a very low heat. Dry-fry a dough disc in the pan for a minute on each side, using a spatula to turn it over. Turn the dough back over again and drizzle a teaspoon of oil around the edges of the pan. Use the spatula to press down and gently flatten the *bhakri* where it puffs up while cooking. Fry for a minute, then flip over and cook the other side for a further minute until golden brown. Remove from the pan and place on a serving plate while you cook the remaining *bhakri*. If you are making them in advance of serving, wrap the cooked *bhakri* in foil to stop them drying out and keep them warm until needed.

Bhakri can be served to accompany any main meal. I find they go particularly well with *chevti dhal* (page 126), *aloo gobi* (page 117), *baath* (page 156) and *murabho* (page 197). Any leftovers can be stored in an airtight container once they've cooled, to be eaten cold the next day (I don't reheat them, as I think it affects the flavour of the *ghee*).

Juvar na rotla –
Healthy sorghum flatbread

(V, WF, OG, N, HO)

Rotla was widely eaten when my mother's generation was growing up; however, it is less popular today. This is a shame, as it is an excellent, healthy bread made with just flour and water, perfect for those watching their weight. Sorghum flour is gluten-free, making this a good option for those who have problems with gluten too. You can cook rotla *in advance of the meal, then just reheat it before serving.*

SERVES 4 (MAKES 8)

300g sorghum flour, plus extra for flouring

Fill a medium bowl with cold water (I use a washing-up bowl) and set it on the work surface near where you will be making the dough.

Put the flour into a large bowl, pour in 250ml of boiling water and mix until the dough starts to come together. While it is still hot, dip your hands into the cold water and knead the dough until smooth, dipping your hands in the water whenever it starts to feel too hot to handle. This dough hardens as it cools, so start preparing the *rotlas* as soon as the dough is smooth and well kneaded (after about 2 minutes).

Divide the dough into 8 roughly equal pieces, then form them into balls between your palms and squash to flatten slightly. Place a flattened dough ball on a lightly floured work surface and roll it into a disc about 15cm in diameter (see method on page 91). If you find that the dough sticks to the work surface, sprinkle a little more flour underneath. Put a flat *tawa* pan or a flat-based non-stick frying pan over a medium heat.

Use a spatula to lift the dough disc into the pan – be careful, as it will be delicate and prone to tearing. Dry-fry the *rotla* for 2 minutes on each side, using the spatula to turn it. Take care not to overcook it, as otherwise it will start to crack. Turn the *rotla* back over again and use the spatula to apply gentle pressure until the underside is light brown, with a few darker speckles. Remove from the pan and place on a serving plate while you roll and cook the remaining *rotlas*. If you are making them in advance of serving, set them aside to cool (simply dry-fry for a couple of minutes on a *tawa* or in a frying pan when needed).

Serve warm, with *sukhu bhinda bataka* (page 124), *khudi* (page193), *mung dhal kichdi* (page 167) and *keri attana* (page 194). You can use any uneaten *rotlas* to make *vagareli rotli* (page 87) for lunch or supper the next day.

Paratha –
Pan-fried chapatti flatbread
(OG, N, HO)

Whenever we go out for an Indian meal, I like to order paratha, *as it is a rich, substantial bread. Paratha comes from northern India and was traditionally eaten at breakfast, but these days it can be enjoyed at any meal. The name comes from the Hindi words 'parat' and 'atta' and roughly translates as 'layers of cooked dough', which is precisely what a good* paratha *should be – multi-layered, flaky and delicious.*

SERVES 4 (MAKES 8)

300 chapatti flour, plus
  8 tablespoons for sprinkling
50ml *ghee* (or clarified butter),
  melted
16 teaspoons sunflower oil,
  plus 8 teaspoons for frying

Sieve the flour into a large bowl, add the *ghee* and stir thoroughly to combine. Pour in 300ml of boiling water and mix with a spoon until the dough comes together and has cooled enough to start using your hands. Knead for 2 minutes, until soft and smooth. Gently smooth the surface with lightly oiled hands, cover with clingfilm and set aside until you are ready to cook the *paratha*.

Divide the dough into 16 roughly equal pieces, then form them into balls between your palms and squash to flatten slightly. Place a flattened dough ball on a lightly floured work surface and roll it into a disc about 19–20cm in diameter (see method on page 91). Roll out a second disc the same size.

Pour 2 teaspoons of oil on to one of the dough discs and spread it over the surface with the back of the spoon, then sprinkle a tablespoon of flour evenly over the oiled dough. Place the second dough disc on top of the oiled-floured disc. Starting with the edge closest to you, roll the two-layered disc up like a large cigar. Fold in half, then use your palms to squash it flat, pressing all the layers together. Lightly flour the work surface and roll into a disc about 19–20cm in diameter again.

Put a flat *tawa* pan or a flat-based non-stick frying pan over a medium heat. Dry-fry the *paratha* for 1 minute, then carefully lift the edge to check that the underside is starting to bubble. Use a spatula to turn it over and dry-fry for a minute on the other side. Turn the *paratha* back over again and drizzle a teaspoon of oil around the edges of the pan. Fry for 30 seconds, then flip over and fry the other side for 30 seconds. Remove from the pan and place on a serving plate while you prepare and cook the remaining *paratha*.

Paratha is delicious with any meal but works particularly well with richer dishes. I like to serve it warm or cold, with *aloo gobi* (page 117), *ghilora reveya* (page 129), mushroom *palak* (page 135) or *kehra na reveya* (page 138). If you are making them in advance of serving, wrap the cooked *paratha* in foil to stop them drying out and keep them warm until needed. Any left over can be stored in an airtight container once they've cooled, to be eaten cold the next day (I don't reheat them, as I think it affects the flavour of the *ghee*).

Puri –
Fried puffy bread

(V, OG, N)

Puri is traditionally served at lavish Indian weddings, either cooked the day before and eaten cold, or fried on the day and served piping hot. The secret to making great puri *lies in two things: kneading the dough thoroughly, and frying it at the correct temperature. If you get these two things right, your* puris *should be wonderfully light and flaky – one of our customers describes them as little clouds floating to the table!*

SERVES 4 (MAKES 16)

300g chapatti flour, sieved
8 teaspoons fine semolina
40ml sunflower oil, plus more
 for deep-frying

Put the flour and semolina into a large bowl and mix well to distribute the semolina evenly through the flour. Add the oil and 250ml of warm water and stir until the dough starts to come together. Knead for at least 2 minutes, until firm and smooth. Cover with lightly oiled clingfilm and set aside to rest for 30 minutes or more (several hours, if need be) in a cool place.

Divide the dough into 16 roughly equal pieces, then form them into balls between your palms and squash to flatten slightly. Place a flattened dough ball on a lightly floured work surface and roll it into a thin disc about 9cm in diameter (see method on page 91). If you find that the dough sticks to the work surface, sprinkle a little more flour underneath. Repeat with the remaining dough balls, placing the discs on a lightly oiled baking sheet as you go, making sure they don't overlap.

Heat the frying oil – about 20cm deep – in a large pan over a high heat (or in a deep fat fryer, if you have one). Test the temperature by dropping a few little pieces of dough into the oil – when it is hot enough, they will quickly float to the surface.

Gently place a couple of *puris* in the oil (I cook 4 at a time, but start with 2 if you haven't done this before). As soon as they puff up, turn them over, then spoon oil over them to help them cook evenly. Fry them for about 30 seconds, until golden brown and puffed full of air. Remove them from the oil with a slotted spoon and leave them to rest on kitchen paper while you fry the next batch. Repeat until all the *puris* have been fried.

Serve hot or cold (I think they are best eaten hot and crispy straight from the pan). *Puri* goes particularly well with rich tomato-based dishes like *paneer masala* (page 142) or *mattar paneer* (page 140). Any left over can be stored in an airtight container once they've cooled and eaten cold the next day with curry – try them with *sukhu bataka* (page 116) – or as a nibble, spread with a generous layer of *murabho* (page 197) or *limbu attana* (page 196), to enjoy with a cup of tea.

Bathura –
Fluffy fried fermented bread

(OG, N)

Bathura is a Punjabi classic – delicious, soft, fluffy fried bread, made with a yoghurt-fermented dough. It is traditionally eaten with chole. Try them together and you'll see why – the combination of spicy, cinnamon-scented chickpeas and the soft chewy bread makes chole bathura a match made in heaven. This bread is wonderful warm or cold – if serving it warm, fry it as the last element in your meal once everything else is ready.

SERVES 4 (MAKES 16)

380g plain flour, sieved
20g *ghee* (or clarified butter), melted
50g plain live set yoghurt
1 teaspoon salt
1 teaspoon black peppercorns, coarsely ground or crushed
200ml soda water
sunflower oil, for frying

Put the flour, *ghee*, yoghurt, salt and pepper into a large bowl and mix to combine. Add the soda water and stir until the dough starts to come together. Knead for at least 2 minutes, until firm. Put the dough into an airtight container and leave for at least 1 hour at room temperature while the fermenting yoghurt works its magic and causes the dough to rise slightly.

Divide the dough into 16 roughly equal pieces. Lightly oil your hands (this makes it easier to handle the sticky dough), then form the dough pieces into balls between your palms and squash to flatten them slightly. Place a flattened dough ball on a clean work surface and roll it into a thin disc about 12cm in diameter (see method on page 91). Repeat with the remaining dough balls, placing the discs on a lightly oiled baking sheet as you go, making sure they don't overlap.

Heat the frying oil – about 20cm deep – in a large pan over a high heat (or in a deep fat fryer, if you have one). Test the temperature by dropping a few little pieces of dough into the oil – when it is hot enough, they will quickly float to the surface.

Gently place a couple of *bathura* in the oil (I cook 3 or 4 at a time, but start with 2 if you haven't done this before). They will start to puff up within about 30 seconds. As soon as they do, turn them over, then spoon oil over them to help them cook evenly. Fry for a further 15 seconds or so until golden brown. Remove from the oil with a slotted spoon and leave to rest on kitchen paper while you fry the next batch. Repeat until all the *bathura* have been fried.

Serve warm or cold, with *chole* (page 132), *mattar paneer* (page 140) or any other rich tomato and onion based curry. Any left over can be stored in an airtight container once they've cooled, to be eaten cold the next day (I don't reheat them, as I think it affects the flavour of the *ghee*).

Mal pura –
Gujarati jaggery bread

(OG, N)

Mal pura is a prime example of rich Gujarati food and one of our most famous breads. Although sweet, it is usually served with curry, as the jaggery balances the spicy, savoury flavours in the rest of the meal. It can also be enjoyed with a cup of tea as a treat for elevenses or as a mid-afternoon pick-me-up. The batter needs to ferment for at least 8 hours, so I make it in advance and leave it overnight.

SERVES 4 (MAKES 20)

200g jaggery, finely chopped
  (or demerara/soft brown sugar)
300g chapatti flour
4 teaspoons *ghee* (or clarified
  butter), melted
1 teaspoon plain live set yoghurt
sunflower oil, for frying
3 tablespoons white
  poppy seeds

Dissolve the jaggery in 400ml of warm water in a medium bowl, then sieve into a jug to remove any sugar cane fibres.

Mix the flour, *ghee* and yoghurt in a large bowl, working the *ghee* and yoghurt into the flour with your fingertips. Add the jaggery solution and whisk to form a smooth, pourable batter. Seal in an airtight container to ferment at room temperature for at least 8 hours, or overnight.

Heat the oil – about 15cm – in a deep pan over a high heat. Test the temperature by sprinkling a few small drops of batter into the oil – when it is hot enough, they will quickly float to the surface.

Drop 2 ladlefuls of batter into the oil, half a ladle at a time. The 4 dollops of batter will sink straight to the bottom of the pan and spread out. Leave to fry for 2 minutes (by which time they have risen to the surface), then turn them over and fry for a further minute until dark golden brown at the edges.

Use a slotted spoon to lift the *mal pura* out of the oil and place one on top of the other on a flat frying sieve or mesh screen (the kind used to stop fat spitting during frying). Use a spatula to press the *mal pura* firmly against the mesh to remove any excess oil. I do this over the oil pan, but be very careful not to drop them back in and splash yourself. If you haven't done this before, you may prefer to rest the flat sieve or mesh screen on kitchen paper on the work surface while you press the *mal pura* on it.

Leave the cooked *mal pura* (which will now be stuck together) to rest on the mesh while you start the next batch frying. After a couple of minutes, separate them, place them on a serving plate and sprinkle with poppy seeds. Repeat until all the batter has been used up.

Serve warm or cold – *mal pura* goes particularly well with *sukhu bataka* (page 116) or *renghan lilva* (page 110). Any left over will keep for a day in an airtight container and will be great with a nice hot cup of *adhu vari chai* (page 228).

Velmi –
Sweet and buttery lentil-filled flatbread

(OG, N)

I confess that I have a naughty sweet tooth and I really enjoy velmi *(also called* vedmi *or* puran puri*). It's very rich, especially when drenched in clarified butter, as is traditional. Mohan always says the sign of a good* velmi *is that the butter runs all the way down to your elbows – at times he can be a very messy eater!*

SERVES 4 (MAKES 8)

8–16 teaspoons *ghee*
  (or clarified butter),
  melted, to serve

Dhal
310g *tuvar dhal* (dried
  pigeon peas/yellow lentils)
1 teaspoon oil
320g jaggery,
  cut into thin flakes (or
  demerara/soft brown sugar)
1 teaspoon cardamom seeds,
  finely ground

Dough
200g chapatti flour
1 tablespoon sunflower oil

Rinse the *tuvar dhal* at least 3 times in hot water (see page 25), then leave to soak in hot water for 15 minutes before draining.

Put the *dhal* and 1 litre of hot water into a large pan over a high heat. Bring to the boil, then simmer over a medium heat for a couple of minutes until it starts to foam. Skim the froth from the surface, add the teaspoon of oil and simmer three-quarters covered for 25 minutes or so, stirring occasionally, until most of the water has evaporated. Reduce the heat to low and cook three-quarters covered for a further 5 minutes, until the *dhal* is soft and cooked through.

Stir the jaggery into the *dhal* and cook uncovered over a high heat, stirring regularly to stop it bubbling and spitting too much as the jaggery dissolves. Continue to simmer and stir until enough water has evaporated to allow the spoon to stand upright in the *dhal* (this should take around 8 minutes). Stir in the cardamom, then remove the pan from the heat and scoop the *dhal* on to a large baking tray, spreading it out and stirring occasionally to help it cool.

Put the chapatti flour, oil and 200ml of boiling water into a large bowl and mix until the dough comes together. Knead for a couple of minutes until you have a firm dough. Rub some oil on your palms and smooth over the surface of the dough, then wrap it in clingfilm to stop it drying out. Leave to rest for 35 minutes or so, until the *dhal* has cooled.

When the *dhal* is cool enough to handle (after about an hour), divide it into 8 equal portions and use your hands to roll each one into a ball. Divide the dough into 8 roughly equal pieces, then form them into balls between your palms and squash to flatten slightly.

Put a flat *tawa* pan or non-stick frying pan over a low heat. Place a flattened dough ball on a lightly floured work surface and roll it into a disc about 7cm in diameter. Put a dhal ball in the middle and gently fold the dough upwards to form a parcel around the filling. Pinch the edges of the dough together where they meet at the top.

Gently press the *dhal*-filled dough ball between your hands to flatten slightly. Place on the work surface with the pinched-together join underneath and carefully roll out again to form a disc about 14cm in diameter. Take your time doing this, as the filled dough will not stand up to being rolled too quickly or vigorously.

Place in the preheated pan and dry-fry for a minute, then turn over to fry the other side. Continue to turn it and cook for a minute on each side until the dough starts to darken slightly and harden (this should take about 4–5 minutes). Remove from the pan and place on kitchen paper while you prepare and cook the remaining *velmi*. If you are making these in advance, wrap the cooked *velmi* in foil until needed, then either reheat for a couple of minutes in the pan before serving, or enjoy cold as a lovely contrast to the hot *ghee*.

To enjoy *velmi* at its buttery best, use a spoon to break the surface, pour in a couple of teaspoons of melted *ghee* or clarified butter, roll up your sleeves, then pick it up and tuck in! Serve with *renghan lilva* (page 110) or *aloo gobi* (page 117), *khudi* (page 193), *baath* (page 156) and *methi safarjan* (page 202). Any left over can be stored in an airtight container once they've cooled, to be eaten cold as a treat the next day with warm *ghee* drizzled over them …

SOUPS, PICKLES, SIDE DISHES, CHUTNEYS AND DIPS

SOUPS, PICKLES, SIDE DISHES, CHUTNEYS AND DIPS

You will always find a sauce-like soup served at any traditional Gujarati meal, along with plenty of pickles, chutneys, dips and side dishes. The type of soup is a matter of personal taste, depending on the other flavours in the meal — there are no hard-and-fast rules, but I tend to make spicy lentil *dhal* when serving steamed *baath* rice, and tangy yoghurt-based *khudi* when serving *pilau* or other spiced rice. Aromatic vegetable and lentil *sambar* soup goes particularly well with *masala dosa*, but is also delicious eaten on its own, or with a little *baath* and some *kopru* coconut dip as a healthy light meal.

Gujarati pickles are used to add a little something to the meal – maybe the tangy bite of green mango *keri attana* or Indian lemon *limbu attana*, or the sweet spice of golden mango *murabho* with its cinnamon and cardamom notes, or the hot crunch of *rai marcha* (pickled green chillies). Indian pickles traditionally use the heat of the sun to speed the pickling process, maturing gently in glass jars – in my youth we would use the old glass bottles from the local sweet shop. As hot sunshine is a bit of a rarity in the UK, even in summer, some pickles demand a little

patience before they are ready to eat, but I promise they are worth the wait.

My husband loves side dishes for the variety in flavours and textures that they add, often enjoying a couple of different pickles, crunchy *sambharo* coleslaw and refreshing *raitu* with his meal. You might prefer *masala kakadhi* (chilli-garlic cucumbers) or perhaps a zesty relish to pep up your palate – the tart green apples in *methi safarjan*, unripe green mangoes in *kachi keri chundo* and sharp green tomatoes in *kacha* tomato relish are perfect for this. If you're looking for something slightly sweeter, try red pepper and carrot *shimla mirch*, or the fresh taste of *safarjan wattana*, with its lovely balance of fresh peas and sour apple.

Fiery garlic and chilli *lasan* chutney, sweet tamarind *imli* chutney and nutty *sing dhania* (sesame-coriander dip) bring an extra dimension and a little richness to many dishes. In contrast, cooling yoghurt dips like *raitu* and minty *phudino dai* help to maintain the balance of flavours and tame the chilli heat in other dishes – useful to know if you don't eat Indian food every day!

SOUPS, PICKLES, SIDE DISHES, CHUTNEYS AND DIPS

Sambar –
Aromatic vegetable and lentil soup

(V, WF, OG, N, HO)

Sambar is traditionally served with masala dosa *(page 145) and originally comes from southern India, but is now enjoyed by people the world over. It is great as a healthy light meal, either on its own as a satisfying soup, or served with* baath *(page 156) and* kopru *dip (page 214).*

SERVES 4–6

200g *tuvar dhal* (split pigeon
  peas/yellow lentils)
1 teaspoon sunflower oil
1 x 400g tin of peeled plum
  tomatoes, finely chopped
  or blended
1 baby aubergine, cut into
  1cm cubes
1 small/medium bottle gourd,
  peeled and cut into 1cm cubes
4cm root ginger,
  peeled and roughly chopped
30g fresh or frozen peas
  (ideally *petits pois*)
2½ teaspoons salt
1 teaspoon turmeric
1 teaspoon medium red
  chilli powder
1 tablespoon granulated sugar
½ teaspoon *garam masala*
1 handful of fresh coriander,
  finely chopped

Tarka (spiced oil)

50ml sunflower oil
1 teaspoon cumin seeds
1 teaspoon brown mustard seeds
¼ teaspoon asafetida
10 fresh curry leaves

Rinse the *tuvar dhal* at least 4 times in hot water (see page 25), then leave to soak in hot water for 15 minutes before draining.

Put the *dhal* into a very large pan and add 1.5 litres of boiling water. Bring to the boil, then simmer over a medium heat for a couple of minutes until it starts to foam. Skim the froth from the surface, add the teaspoon of oil and simmer three-quarters covered for a further 28–30 minutes, stirring occasionally, until the *dhal* is soft and cooked through.

Add the tomatoes, bring the mixture back to the boil, and simmer three-quarters covered again over a medium heat for 2–3 minutes, stirring every minute or so. Remove from the heat and blitz with a hand-held blender until the mixture has a really smooth texture.

Return the pan with the blended *dhal*/tomato mixture to a medium heat. Stir in the cubes of aubergine and bottle gourd along with another 500ml of boiling water, then leave to cook uncovered for 2–3 minutes. While it is cooking, crush the ginger using a pestle and mortar (or a blender), to make a fine pulp.

Stir the ginger, peas, salt, turmeric, chilli powder, sugar, *garam masala* and chopped coriander into the *dhal* mixture. Leave to simmer gently, uncovered, for 4–5 minutes while you prepare the *tarka*.

Heat the sunflower oil in a small pan over a medium heat for about 30 seconds, then add the cumin seeds. When they start to darken (after about 30 seconds), tip in the mustard seeds, and as soon as they start to pop, add the asafetida. Add the curry leaves (be careful, as they will sizzle and spit), then slowly and carefully pour in a ladleful of the lentil/vegetable mixture, a little at a time – do this at arm's length, as the hot *tarka* will spit. Stir, then pour the contents of the small pan into the pan containing the rest of the lentil mixture and stir again.

Bring the *sambar* to the boil and simmer for 10–12 minutes, partially covered, over a low heat, stirring occasionally. Remove from the heat, cover the pan and leave to rest for 15 minutes to allow the flavours to develop.

Reheat to boiling before serving, making sure you stir well, as some of the deliciousness will be at the bottom of the pan. Any leftovers can be stored in an airtight container in the fridge for a couple of days, to be reheated with a little extra water and enjoyed as a speedy lunch or supper.

Dhal –
Traditional yellow lentil soup

(V, WF, OG, N, HO)

Sweet, spicy dhal *makes a wonderfully rich sauce to accompany* baath *(page 156), and is often served at celebratory meals and festivals. Soothing, satisfying, and a great source of easily digestible protein, it can also be eaten on its own as a light meal.*

SERVES 4

200g *tuvar dhal* (dried pigeon peas/ yellow lentils)
1 teaspoon sunflower oil
1 x 400g tin of peeled plum tomatoes, finely chopped or blended
4cm root ginger, peeled and roughly chopped
2 teaspoons salt
1 teaspoon turmeric
1 teaspoon medium red chilli powder
60g jaggery, cut into thin flakes (or demerara/soft brown sugar)
1 handful of fresh coriander, finely chopped

Tarka (spiced oil)
50ml sunflower oil
2 dried red chillies, snapped in half
1 teaspoon cumin seeds
1 teaspoon brown mustard seeds
¼ teaspoon asafetida

Rinse the *tuvar dhal* at least 4 times in hot water (see page 25), then leave to soak in hot water for 15 minutes to soften before draining.

Put the *dhal* into a very large pan and add 2 litres of boiling water. Bring to the boil, then simmer over a medium heat for a couple of minutes until it starts to foam. Skim the froth from the surface, add the teaspoon of oil and simmer three-quarters covered for about 25 minutes, stirring occasionally, until the *dhal* is soft and cooked through.

Add the tomatoes and another litre of boiling water. Bring the mixture back to the boil, then simmer three-quarters covered over a medium heat for 3–4 minutes. Remove from the heat and blitz with a hand-held blender until the mixture has a really smooth texture, using a spatula to scoop any unblitzed *dhal* from the sides of the pan. Return to a medium heat and simmer gently, uncovered, while you prepare the spices and seasoning.

Crush the ginger using a pestle and mortar (or a blender), to make a fine pulp. Stir the ginger, salt, turmeric, chilli powder, jaggery and chopped coriander into the *dhal* mixture.

Heat the sunflower oil for the *tarka* in a small pan over a medium heat for about 30 seconds, then add the red chillies and cumin seeds. When the cumin seeds start to turn darker brown (after about 30 seconds), add the mustard seeds. As soon as the mustard seeds start to pop, add the asafetida.

Slowly and carefully pour a ladleful of the *dhal* into the *tarka*, a little at a time – do this at arm's length, as the hot *tarka* will spit. Stir, then pour the contents of the *tarka* pan into the pan containing the rest of the *dhal* mixture and stir again.

Bring the *dhal* back to the boil and simmer for 3–4 minutes, then remove from the heat. Leave to rest, covered, for at least 20 minutes to allow the flavours to develop. Reheat to boiling before serving, stirring well to mix in the magic from the bottom of the pan.

Khudi –
Spiced yoghurt soup

(WF, OG, N, HO)

Also known as kadhi *or* karhi, khudi *is a light, tangy sauce to serve with the rice that invariably forms part of any Gujarati meal. Fresh turmeric and white turmeric root can be used in much the same way as root ginger in cooking, although white turmeric can be harder to find, as it is seasonal (if you can't get hold of any – just leave it out, as there'll be plenty of flavour from the other spices).*

SERVES 4

425g plain live set yoghurt
1 tablespoon chickpea flour, sieved
1¼ teaspoons salt
1 tablespoon sugar

Masala

1 fresh green chilli, seeds left in
1cm turmeric root, peeled and
  roughly chopped
8cm white turmeric root (*amba haldi*),
  peeled and roughly chopped
6 fresh curry leaves
1 handful of fresh coriander,
  finely chopped
¼ teaspoon cumin seeds

Tarka (spiced oil)

50ml sunflower oil
1 dried red chilli, snapped in half
1 teaspoon cumin seeds
1 teaspoon brown mustard seeds
10 fresh curry leaves
1 handful of fresh coriander,
  finely chopped

Crush the chilli, turmeric, white turmeric, curry leaves, fresh coriander and cumin seeds together using a pestle and mortar (or a blender), to make a fine masala paste.

Whisk the yoghurt and chickpea flour together in a large pan to combine, then add 500ml of cold water and whisk (or blitz with a hand-held blender) until smooth. Place over a medium heat and stir in the masala paste, salt and sugar. Cook for 4–5 minutes, stirring continuously to ensure that the yoghurt doesn't split, then remove from the heat.

Heat the oil in a small pan or frying pan for 30 seconds over a medium heat, then add the red chilli. Once it starts to turn darker (after about 30 seconds), add the cumin and mustard seeds. As soon as the mustard seeds start to pop, add the curry leaves (be careful, as they will sizzle and spit) and then the coriander.

Slowly and carefully pour a ladleful of the yoghurt mixture into the *tarka*, a little at a time – it's best to do this at arm's length, as the hot *tarka* will spit. Stir, then pour the contents of the *tarka* pan into the pan containing the rest of the yoghurt mixture and stir again.

Remove from the heat and leave to rest, covered, for at least 10 minutes. Once cooled, store in the fridge until needed (I prepare it up to 5 hours in advance of eating).

When you are ready to eat, gently reheat the *khudi* over a medium heat, stirring occasionally, and bring to the boil before serving. Be careful not to leave it cooking for too long, as the longer you heat it, the thicker it becomes. *Khudi* goes wonderfully with *renghan reveya* (page 108), *renghan bataka* (page 111), *bhinda* (page 134), *ghuvar* (page 123), mushroom *palak* (page 135), *mung dhal kichdi* (page 167) or *tuvar dhal kichdi* (page 168).

Keri attana –
Green mango and fenugreek pickle

(V, WF, OG, N)

Pickle is as vital to the full traditional Gujarati meal as rice – it's an absolute must. This one is mouth-wateringly good. I make it from late March to mid-April, during the early part of the mango season when the baby mangoes are about the size of golfballs. This delicious pickle, also known as keri athanu *or* achar, *keeps well for up to 6 months in an airtight sterilized glass jar.*

MAKES 30 SERVINGS
(makes enough to fill a 1 litre glass preserving jar)

194

300ml groundnut oil,
  plus 150–200ml to seal
10 golfball-sized young green
  (unripe) mangoes
150g crushed fenugreek seeds
  (*bardho/bardo*)
100g coarse red chilli powder
  (*resam/resham patti*)
80g salt
50g turmeric
1 teaspoon asafetida

Heat 300ml of groundnut oil in a medium pan over a high heat until it starts to smoke slightly, then remove from the heat and leave to cool for at least an hour. This heating and cooling helps to release the flavour of the oil and makes it better for preserving.

Preheat the oven to 100°C/80°C fan/gas mark ¼ while you wash the jar, then pop it into the oven for 10 minutes to dry and sterilize it. Stand the jar upside down on a clean tea towel until needed.

Wipe the mangoes with a damp cloth, then cut lengthways into quarters, leaving the last couple of centimetres at the stem end intact to hold them together. The stone inside baby mangoes is still soft enough to cut through, so don't worry about having to work around it.

Put the fenugreek, chilli powder, salt, turmeric and asafetida into a wide shallow bowl and stir. Make a well in the middle of the spice mix, pour in the cooled groundnut oil and stir together until all the spices are thoroughly worked in and you have a thick but workable mixture.

Stuff the cut mangoes with the spice mixture – fill them as full as possible, while taking care not to overdo it and split them (although if the odd one does split, don't worry too much, it'll still taste fine). Gently place the stuffed mangoes in the sterilized glass jar, then tip in any remaining mixture.

Pour 150–200ml of groundnut oil over the stuffed mangoes to seal them, making sure they are only just covered – don't be tempted to pour in too much oil, as it may cause the spices to leach away from the mangoes. Close the jar lid firmly to ensure that it is airtight.

Leave to mature for at least 2 weeks in a cool dark place – I keep my pickles in the garage. The longer you leave them, the better the flavour and the more tender the finished pickle will be.

Keri attana goes well with any meal where you are serving *dhal* and rice as accompaniments to the main dish, and it is particularly good with *aloo gobi paratha* (page 94), *sukhu bataka* (page 116) or *tuvar dhal kichdi* (page 168).

To serve, remove the number of mangoes you need from the jar and cut each one into 8 strips – I generally work on the basis of 2 strips per person at a main meal. Serve the strips in a small dish or bowl, mixed with a good helping of the marinade.

OPPOSITE
top left:
Limbu attana (page 196)
bottom left:
Murabho (page 197)
right:
Keri attana (page 194)

Limbu attana –
Sweet and sour Indian lemon pickle

(V, WF, OG, N)

This classic Gujarati pickle (sometimes called nimbu achar*) goes beautifully with many traditional dishes, and also works brilliantly with a cheese board. Indian lemons are smaller and rounder than Mediterranean lemons, and have a much thinner skin, so if you can't get hold of Indian lemons, try using limes instead. These spicy lemons aren't quick to make – you need to allow at least 4 weeks from the start of the process to the first tasting – but they are well worth the effort, and they keep for up to 12 months in airtight sterilized jars. Don't worry if they turn a little darker as they age – the colour will deepen as the flavours develop.*

MAKES ENOUGH TO FILL 3 x 500ML GLASS JARS

1kg small Indian lemons,
   quartered, with pips removed
100g salt
50g turmeric
750g granulated sugar
50g mustard powder
70g coarse red chilli powder
   (*resam/resham patti*)
1 teaspoon asafetida

Put the quartered lemons, salt and turmeric into a large plastic container with an airtight lid. Seal the lid on, then gently shake the jar. Leave them in a cool place for 3 weeks to soften and marinate, giving them a gentle shake each morning to toss the lemons in the salt, turmeric and lemon juice.

THREE WEEKS LATER

Drain the lemons and discard the marinade. Put the sugar into a large pan with 300ml of cold water and heat for a minute over a medium heat, stirring continuously. Stir in the lemons and simmer uncovered for 15 minutes, stirring occasionally.

Stir in the mustard, chilli powder and asafetida and simmer for a further 8–10 minutes, stirring all the while. If you have missed any pips, they will float to the surface as the lemons cook – scoop them out, otherwise they will add a bitter taste to the pickle. Remove from the heat, allow to cool, then cover and leave to marinate for at least 24 hours.

Pour the cooled lemon pickle into the sterilized glass jars, making sure the lids are firmly closed to ensure that they are airtight. Leave to mature for at least 1 week in a cool dark place – the longer you leave them, the better the flavour and the more tender the finished pickle will be.

Limbu attana is great with *vagarela baath* (page 86), *sukhu bhinda bataka* (page 124), *thepla* (page 91) or *mung dhal kichdi* (page 167), delicious spread on cold *puri* (page 177) to eat as a snack, and fantastic instead of shop-bought pickle with some good strongly flavoured cheese!

Murabho –
Cinnamon and cardamom-infused sweet mango pickle

(V, WF, OG, N)

While discussing which recipes should go into this book, I served murabho *to our beloved editor. She loved its depth of flavour and insisted it was included. This is delicious with tikki puri (page 96) or any kind of bread – bhakri (page 172), paratha (page 174), puri (page 177), rotli (page 170) – whether as part of a main meal or just on its own, like mango marmalade! I make this with totapuri mangoes, but you can use any firm semi-ripe mangoes.*

MAKES ABOUT 500ML

200g granulated sugar
500g medium-ripe (light yellow)
  mangoes, peeled and grated in
  long strands
12cm cinnamon stick,
  broken into 1cm pieces
12 cloves
12 cardamom pods

Preheat the oven to 100°C/80°C fan/gas mark ¼ while you wash a few glass jars, then pop them into the oven for 10 minutes to dry and sterilize them. Stand them upside down on a clean tea towel until you need them.

Tip the sugar and grated mango into a large pan and gently stir for about 5 minutes until all the sugar has dissolved in the mango juice.

Place the pan over a very low heat for 20 minutes, stirring continuously. During this time the mixture will slowly come to a gentle simmer and gradually change from clear to cloudy in appearance. Stir in the spices and simmer for a further 5 minutes, stirring all the while.

Remove from the heat and transfer to a heatproof bowl or pan. Set aside to cool, stirring occasionally, then cover and leave to cool completely overnight.

Scoop the cooled *murabho* into the sterilized glass jars, making sure the lids are firmly closed to ensure that they are airtight. This mouth-watering sweet mango pickle will keep for up to 2 months.

Rai marcha –
Pickled green chillies with mustard seeds

(V, WF, OG, N, HO)

My son Mayur loves these moreish pickled chillies with crushed yellow mustard seeds. They are perfect to add a hot and spicy crunch to any festive family meal. I find that Ghanaian chillies are best for this pickle, as they are crisp but not too hot.

MAKES 20

20 fresh green chillies
 (each roughly 10cm long)
100g split yellow mustard seeds
 (*rai bhardo*)
½ teaspoon turmeric
1 teaspoon salt
1 teaspoon granulated sugar
50ml lemon juice
50ml sunflower oil

Wash the chillies and slice along their length to open them, leaving the stem and seeds intact.

Put all the other ingredients into a medium bowl and mix thoroughly, making sure the mustard seeds are fully coated in oil and lemon.

Carefully stuff the chillies with the spiced marinade. Place in an airtight plastic container, top with any remaining marinade and seal the lid on. Leave in the fridge to marinate for at least a couple of hours (or up to a couple of days, if preparing in advance of a lunch or dinner party), to allow the flavours to combine and develop before serving.

These go beautifully with *dhokra* (page 62), or any main meal where you fancy a little extra chilli kick. They will keep for up to a week in an airtight container in the fridge, although in our house there are never any left after the second day!

Masala kakadhi – Chilli-garlic cucumbers

(V, WF, N, HO)

As soon as the rainy season starts in India, cucumbers start sprouting in all the gardens, and masala kakadhi *(or* kakdi*) starts to appear at every meal. It's easy to make, tasty and refreshing to eat.*

SERVES 4

4 baby cucumbers (or
  1 large cucumber, quartered)
1 teaspoon salt
lemon wedges, to serve

Masala

1–2 fresh green chillies,
  seeds left in
2–4 cloves of garlic
pinch of salt

Crush the chillies and garlic together with a pinch of salt using a pestle and mortar (or a blender), to make a fine masala paste.

Cut the cucumbers lengthways into quarters, leaving the last 2–3cm at the stem end intact to hold them together. Gently open them and spread ¼ teaspoon of salt on the cut surfaces of each cucumber. Holding the cucumbers over the sink one at a time, gently squeeze and twist them to wring the water out of them. The salt will help them release the water, so take your time and get as much moisture out as possible.

Spread a quarter of the masala paste on the cut surfaces of each cucumber, then twist each one a few times to work the masala in and infuse the cucumber with flavour.

Serve immediately, with lemon wedges to squeeze over them, alongside any meal of curry, *rotli* and rice. They are particularly good with *aloo gobi* (page 117), *tarka dhal* (page 143), *mattar paneer* (page 140) or *lila dhania baath* (page 154).

Sambharo –
Chilli, carrot, cabbage and pepper salad

(V, WF, OG, N, HO)

Often served at traditional Indian wedding feasts, the hot, tangy taste of this Gujarati version of coleslaw makes it a versatile side dish to eat with any meal.

SERVES 4

½ small cabbage, grated
  (into roughly 6cm long shreds)
1 medium carrot, finely sliced
  (into roughly 6cm long shreds)
½ green pepper, deseeded and
  finely sliced
½ red pepper, deseeded and
  finely sliced
50ml sunflower oil
½ teaspoon brown mustard seeds
2–4 fresh green chillies, finely
  sliced and seeds left in
¼ teaspoon salt
1 tablespoon lemon juice

Put the cabbage, carrot and peppers into a salad bowl and gently mix with your hands.

Heat the oil in a small pan for 30 seconds over a medium heat, then add the mustard seeds. When they start to pop, stir in the sliced chillies and immediately remove from the heat. Stir in the salt and lemon juice.

Pour over the chopped vegetables and mix together, using your hands or salad servers to toss the vegetables and coat them in the spicy oil. Place the salad bowl on the table with the rest of the meal, so that people can help themselves.

Sambharo will keep in an airtight container in the fridge for a day, but is best eaten fresh to enjoy the crunch of the vegetables in the warm spicy dressing.

Methi safarjan –
Fenugreek, chilli and apple relish

(V, WF, OG, N, HO)

When I first moved to the UK in 1965 and was living with my uncle in Loughborough, we couldn't get hold of many Indian vegetables, and exotic fruits like mangoes were nowhere to be found. One day I bought a cooking apple – very, very sour but perfect as a substitute for unripe green mangoes. With it, I was able to create this relish, and Sunday dinner was saved!

SERVES 8

25g fenugreek seeds, coarsely crushed
1 teaspoon turmeric
¼ teaspoon asafetida
½ teaspoon salt
2 teaspoons coarse red chilli powder (*resam/resham patti*)
25ml sunflower oil
1 large Bramley or other sour cooking apple, chopped into 2cm cubes

Mix the fenugreek, turmeric, asafetida, salt, chilli powder and oil together in a medium bowl, rubbing the mixture between your fingers and thumb to work all the spices together, then use a spoon to stir in the chopped apple.

This relish goes particularly well with *baath* (page 156) and *khudi* (page 193), so serve it alongside these to accompany dishes like *renghan reveya* (page 108) or *bhinda* (page 134). You can serve it straight away or store it in an airtight container in the fridge for a day or two. The longer you leave it, the softer the apple becomes. I like it to have a good crunch, so I tend to make *methi safarjan* just before I want to serve it.

Lila dhania lasan –
Coriander, chilli and garlic relish

(V, WF, N, HO)

In my constant quest to create new flavour combinations, I created this recipe when thinking of new dips for my daughter Hina's seventh birthday – given that she's married with her own family now, you can tell that this is a recipe with staying power! This relish will keep in the fridge for 10 days or so in an airtight container.

MAKES ABOUT 200ML

3–4 handfuls of fresh coriander
4–6 cloves of garlic
1–3 fresh green chillies,
    seeds left in
1 teaspoon cumin seeds
1 teaspoon salt
1 teaspoon granulated sugar
5 teaspoons lemon juice
4 teaspoons sunflower oil
juice of 1 Indian lemon
    (or a lime), to serve

Preheat the oven to 100°C/80°C fan/gas mark ¼ while you wash a glass jar, then pop it into the oven for 10 minutes to dry and sterilize it. Stand it upside down on a clean tea towel until needed.

Put the coriander, garlic, chillies, cumin seeds, salt, sugar and lemon juice into a blender and blitz to a fine pulp. I shake the blender while blitzing and stop three or four times to open the top and use a spatula to push the mixture back down the sides to make sure everything is blended together.

Scoop the lovely deep green mixture into a small bowl, add the sunflower oil and mix it in. Spoon into the sterilized glass jar, making sure the lid is firmly closed to ensure that it's airtight. Store in the fridge until needed.

To help revitalize the colour and bring a fresh tang to the relish, squeeze in the Indian lemon juice just before serving alongside Prashad spring rolls (page 44), *bataka vada* (page 46), *kakdi na panella* (page 64), *tikki puri* (page 96) or *renghan reveya* (page 108), or as a vital ingredient in my flavoursome *bhel* recipe (page 98).

Kachi keri chundo –
Green mango and onion relish

(V, WF, N, HO)

This is one of my husband's favourite side dishes. It is almost like a palate cleanser between mouthfuls – sharp and fresh. If you can't get hold of baby mangoes, use small ordinary mangoes, but make sure they are really unripe.

SERVES 4

½ medium onion,
  roughly chopped
1 teaspoon cumin seeds
2 medium green (unripe)
  baby mangoes
2 fresh green chillies, seeds left in
2 cloves of garlic
1 tablespoon granulated sugar
1 teaspoon salt

Blitz the onion and cumin in a blender until the onion is roughly chopped.

Peel the mangoes, destone and cut into chunks. Add the mangoes, chillies, garlic, sugar and salt to the chopped onions in the blender and blitz to a grainy pulp, pausing as necessary to use a spatula to push down any relish which starts to climb the sides.

Refrigerate in an airtight container until you are ready to serve. This relish will keep for 3–4 days in the fridge and goes well with pretty much everything; however, Mohan particularly likes to eat it with *ratalu* (page 137), *dhal* (page 192) and *baath* (page 156).

Shimla mirch ~
Red pepper and carrot relish

(V, WF, N, HO)

This is a warm yet delicate relish that works well with starters. I always make this at Christmas when I want to add something red to our dishes. It will keep in an airtight container in the fridge for 2–3 days.

SERVES 4–6

1 teaspoon cumin seeds
1 small carrot, cut into 6 pieces
1 clove of garlic
1 fresh green chilli, seeds left in
¾ teaspoon salt
2 teaspoons granulated sugar
1 medium red pepper, deseeded
  and cut into 8 pieces
4 teaspoons white vinegar

Dry-roast the cumin seeds in a frying pan over a low heat – gently shake the pan and when they start to turn dark brown, remove from the heat, tip into a small bowl and leave to cool for 3–5 minutes.

Blitz the carrot for a few seconds in a blender to break it down to a coarse texture. Add the roasted cumin seeds and all the other ingredients and blitz again to a medium-coarse pulp. Pour into a small bowl and serve straight away, or cover and chill until needed.

This relish is fantastic with *pethis* (page 52), *wattana ni kachori* (page 50), *bheta patra* (page 54), *handvo* (page 60) or *hara bara* kebab (page 65).

Kacha tomato –
Tangy green tomato relish

(V, WF, N, HO)

This is a really refreshingly sharp relish. I make just enough to use on the day, as it tastes best when freshly made.

SERVES 4

3 medium green (unripe)
  tomatoes, quartered
1 handful of fresh coriander,
  finely chopped
1 teaspoon cumin seeds
¾ teaspoon salt
2 teaspoons granulated sugar
1 fresh green chilli, seeds left in
1 clove of garlic

Put all the ingredients into a blender and blitz to a coarse texture. I shake the blender to move the mixture down the sides so that everything is whizzed together, but take care not to purée it, as good-sized tomato chunks bring a fresh burst of flavour.

You can serve this straight away – it goes extremely well with vegetable *pakora* (page 40), *bataka vada* (page 46), *dhal vada* (page 48), *kehra na reveya* (page 138) or *wattana ni kachori* (page 50) – or store in an airtight container in the fridge for a couple of days.

Safarjan wattana – Apple and pea chutney

(V, WF, N, HO)

From the very first day we opened Prashad, it was my aim to do things the way I do at home. 'Fresh and fantastic' is my mantra, and it's perfectly reflected in this fantastic, fresh-flavoured combination of sweet garden peas and sour apple. It will keep for up to a week in an airtight jar in the fridge.

MAKES ABOUT 400ML

100g fresh or frozen peas
½ large cooking apple, cored and cut into 1cm cubes
1–2 handfuls of fresh coriander
1 tablespoon ground cumin
1 teaspoon salt
2½ teaspoons granulated sugar
1–2 fresh green chillies, seeds left in
1–3 cloves of garlic
30g *sev* (Indian vermicelli)
1 tablespoon lemon juice

Preheat the oven to 100°C/80°C fan/gas mark ¼ while you wash a large glass jar, then pop it into the oven for 10 minutes to dry and sterilize it. Stand it upside down on a clean tea towel until needed.

If using frozen peas, rinse them in warm water to start them thawing. Blitz the peas, apple and coriander to a medium coarse texture in a blender or food processor. Add the remaining ingredients and blitz together to a coarse, slightly runny texture.

Scoop into the sterilized glass jar, making sure the lid is firmly closed to ensure that it is airtight. Store in the fridge until needed.

Safarjan wattana goes extremely well with *marcha na bhajia* (page 38), *kandha na bhajia* (page 41), *bataka bhajia* (page 36), Gujarati mixed vegetable samosas (page 42), *pethis* (page 52), *dhal vada* (page 48) or *dhokra* (page 62).

Lasan chutney –
Garlic and red chilli chutney

(V, WF, N, HO)

Lasan is a real gem of a chutney and is the finishing jewel in my streetside chaat dishes. Stored in an airtight container in the fridge, it will keep for up to 6 weeks. And don't think you can only use it with Indian food – used sparingly or in dilution, this flavoursome chutney is perfect for chilli-lovers to add a fiery boost to pizza toppings, and even to pep up sandwiches for packed lunches.

MAKES ABOUT 550ML

50g garlic (13–14 cloves)
100ml lemon juice
50g medium red chilli powder
2½ teaspoons salt

Preheat the oven to 100°C/80°C fan/gas mark ¼ while you wash a couple of jam jars, then pop them into the oven for 10 minutes to dry and sterilize them. Stand them upside down on a clean tea towel until you need them.

Blitz the garlic in a blender until roughly chopped, then add the lemon juice and blitz again until you have a grainy pulp. Add the chilli powder, salt and 200ml of cold water and blitz for a third time until the mixture is lovely and smooth.

Tip the chutney into a mixing bowl, making sure you scoop every last drop out, then add another 200ml of cold water and stir gently.

Pour into the sterilized glass jars, making sure the lids are firmly closed to ensure that they are airtight. Store in the fridge to serve with *chaat* (page 79) or *bhel* (page 98), or simply to use whenever you find yourself in need of a garlicky chilli kick.

Imli chutney –
Sweet and tangy tamarind chutney

(V, WF, OG, N)

I can confidently say that it is the rich deep flavour of my imli *chutney that makes all my streetside snacks so popular. The Prashad recipe has been a closely guarded family secret until now, but I've decided that this is the perfect opportunity to share it. If you want to make a larger batch, just double the amounts below. This chutney will keep for up to 3 weeks in an airtight container in the fridge.*

MAKES ABOUT 400ML

100g dried tamarind
  (from a block), broken into
  4cm square pieces
75g stoned dates, broken into large
  chunks (roughly 2cm long)
50g jaggery, cut into thin flakes
  (or demerara/soft brown sugar)
50g granulated sugar
¾ teaspoon salt
1 teaspoon medium red chilli powder
1 teaspoon ground cumin

Preheat the oven to 100°C/80°C fan/gas mark ¼ while you wash a couple of glass jars, then pop them into the oven for 10 minutes to dry and sterilize them. Stand them upside down on a clean tea towel until you need them.

Put the tamarind, dates, jaggery and sugar into a large pan. Pour in 1.5 litres of boiling water and cook over a high heat for 25 minutes. Stir frequently and scrape down the sides to make sure nothing scorches or burns. Once the mixture has reduced down to a thick flavoursome sauce, remove from the heat and set aside to cool, stirring occasionally. This can take up to 2 hours, but you can halve this by setting the pan in a sinkful of cold water and stirring frequently to aid the cooling process.

Sieve the cooled chutney into a large bowl. Add the salt, chilli powder and ground cumin and blitz with a blender (or whisk). Then stir cold water through until you reach your preferred texture and thickness – 60ml will make it very slightly runny, which is how I like my *imli* chutney, but you may prefer to use more or less than this.

Pour into the sterilized glass jars, making sure the lids are firmly closed to ensure that they are airtight. Store in the fridge to serve with *chaat* (page 79), *dai vada* (page 84), *kakra bhajia* (page 39) or *bhel* (page 98).

Phudino dai – Yoghurt and mint dip

(WF, OG, N, HO)

Most Indian restaurants have a mint and yoghurt dip of some kind as part of their pickle tray, to be enjoyed with poppadoms. I developed mine to have a little chilli kick, so that it is warming and cooling at the same time. I love to use Colman's mint sauce for my phudino dai, *because it gives it a fresh tangy flavour.*

SERVES 4

250g plain live set yoghurt
2 teaspoons mint sauce
¼ teaspoon medium red chilli powder
¼ teaspoon salt
¼ teaspoon granulated sugar

Put all the ingredients into a medium bowl and use a spoon to mix thoroughly but gently – you need to break the yoghurt down to a smooth texture but without being so vigorous that it becomes completely liquid.

Serve immediately, or store in an airtight container in the fridge for a day or two (you will need to give it a good stir before serving). I serve this dip with *methi ni bhaji na bhajia* (page 34), *vegetable pakora* (page 40), *jeera baath* (page 158), *aloo gobi* (page 117) or *paneer masala* (page 142).

VARIATION – PHUDINO KANDHA (MINT AND ONION YOGHURT)

Bobby loves to eat *phudino kandha* with *chole*, as he finds that the creamy mint and onion dip perfectly complements the rich deep flavours of the chickpea curry.

Mix 300g of yoghurt and 3 teaspoons of mint sauce with the same amounts of chilli, salt and sugar as for *phudino dai*. Cover and refrigerate until needed. Shortly before serving, slice a medium onion into thin rings and stir into the minty yoghurt.
Perfect with *chole* (page 132), *makai* (page 121) or *vegetable handi* (page 144).

Kakadhi raitu – Cool cucumber and yoghurt dip

(WF, N, HO)

Raitu plays a vital role in traditional Gujarati cuisine, mainly because the yoghurt helps to balance and neutralize the chilli and spices in the other dishes. There are many different kinds of raitu *and no hard-and-fast rules about what you put in them, but simple, refreshing cucumber* raitu *is a very good place to start . . .*

SERVES 4

1 medium cucumber
300g plain live set yoghurt
¼ teaspoon salt
¼ teaspoon granulated sugar
½ teaspoon ground cumin
pinch of turmeric
1 small/medium carrot, grated

Masala
1 fresh green chilli, seeds left in
1 clove of garlic
pinch of salt

Crush the chilli and garlic together with a pinch of salt using a pestle and mortar (or a blender), to make a fine masala paste.

Rinse the cucumber, then grate it into a colander in the sink. Using your hands, squeeze the grated cucumber firmly to remove as much water from it as you can.

Put the masala paste, yoghurt, salt, sugar and spices into a medium bowl and mix thoroughly but gently to break the yoghurt down to a smooth texture – take care not to be so vigorous that it becomes completely liquid. Gently fold in the grated cucumber and carrot.

Serve immediately, or cover and store in the fridge for up to 2 hours. Remember that the longer the *raitu* sits, the more watery it becomes (as the cucumber releases more liquid), so stir well before serving. This goes particularly well with *bataka bhajia* (page 212), *paneer tikka* (page 69), *Bombay bataka* (page 113), *chevti dhal* (page 126) or *baath* (page 156).

VARIATION – KANDHA RAITU – ONION AND YOGHURT DIP

Omit the carrot and cucumber, and instead use 1 medium onion, chopped into small chunks. Serve with *sukhu bhinda bataka* (page 124) or *paneer masala* (page 142).

VARIATION –MURA RAITU – RADISH AND YOGHURT DIP

Omit the carrot and cucumber, and instead use 8 radishes, cut into 2mm-wide slices. This is delicious with *ferar bataka* (page 115) or *valor ajmo* (page 128).

OPPOSITE – top: *Kakadhi raitu* (page 212); right: *Kopru* (page 214); left: *Sing dhania* (page 215)

Kopru –
Mustard seed, curry leaf and coconut dip

(WF, OG, N, HO)

This makes a perfect addition to any meal, although originally I created it to go with my south Indian dishes. My version includes yoghurt, which is not strictly the way it would be made in south India, but as you will have realized by now, I always like to add my own twist. I make this before I start cooking the rest of the meal, so that it has a good long time to chill in the fridge before serving. The chilling helps the flavours to come together and keeps the texture of the dip nice and firm. Plus ice-cold kopru *is the perfect refreshing foil for steaming hot* sambar *and crispy filled* masala dosa ...

SERVES 4

425g plain live set yoghurt
70g coarse unsweetened
  desiccated coconut
½ teaspoon salt
2 teaspoons granulated sugar
2 handfuls of fresh coriander,
  finely chopped
2 fresh green chillies, seeds left in
75ml sunflower oil
1 teaspoon brown mustard seeds
1 teaspoon cumin seeds
10 fresh curry leaves

Tip the yoghurt into a medium bowl and stir to break it down to a smooth texture. Stir in the coconut, salt and sugar.

Put half the chopped coriander into a blender with the chillies and blitz to a medium coarse texture. Scoop into the yoghurt mixture and stir.

Heat the oil in a small pan for 1 minute over a medium heat, then add the mustard seeds and cumin seeds. When the mustard seeds start to pop, add the curry leaves and the rest of the chopped coriander (be careful, as the leaves will sizzle and spit as they meet the oil) and stir. Remove the pan from the heat.

Pour the spiced oil into the yoghurt mixture and stir to combine. Cover with clingfilm and store in the refrigerator until you are ready to serve, so that it will be lovely and cold when you come to eat it.

Kopru goes wonderfully with most dishes, but I like to serve it with *bafela patra* (page 57) or alongside *masala dosa* (page 145) and *sambar* (page 190). Any left over can be stored in an airtight container in the fridge for a couple of days.

Sing dhania –
Sesame, peanut and coriander dip

(V, WF, HO)

This recipe was taught to me by my auntie, who loved the nutty flavour of the peanuts and sesame alongside the fresh clean taste of the coriander. She was passionate about food and amazingly meticulous – for example, when she picked runner beans from the garden for the evening meal, she would make sure they were all exactly the same length! This dip keeps well for up to 5 days in an airtight container in the fridge.

MAKES ABOUT 275ML

100g red-skinned
  (unsalted, unroasted) peanuts
20g sesame seeds
2–4 fresh green chillies, seeds left in
2–4 cloves of garlic
1½ teaspoons cumin seeds
1 teaspoon salt
1 teaspoon granulated sugar
3–4 handfuls of fresh coriander,
  roughly chopped
4 teaspoons lemon juice
4 tablespoons sunflower oil

Preheat the oven to 100°C/80°C fan/gas mark ¼ while you wash a glass jar, then pop it into the oven for 10 minutes to dry and sterilize it. Stand it upside down on a clean tea towel until you need it.

Blitz the peanuts to a fine texture in a blender or food processor, then tip into a medium bowl. Put the sesame seeds, chillies, garlic, cumin seeds, salt, sugar and coriander into the blender and blitz to a coarse texture. Add to the bowl of finely ground peanuts and mix well. Return the mixture to the blender, add 25ml of cold water and blitz again to a fine grainy texture. Scoop back into the bowl again and stir in the lemon juice and oil.

Pour into the sterilized glass jar, making sure the lid is firmly closed to ensure that it is airtight. Store in the fridge until needed.

Serve as part of a main meal, to accompany *Bombay bataka* (page 113) and *rotli* (page 170), or *desi chana* (page 131) and *baath* (page 156).

DRINKS, DESSERTS
AND SWEETS

DRINKS, DESSERTS AND SWEETS

We Gujaratis are known throughout India for our sweet tooth – we like to add a little sugar or jaggery to balance the flavours in our *dhal*, curries and other main dishes, and we love to make puddings to enjoy at mealtimes and sweet treats to nibble as an indulgent mid-morning or mid-afternoon snack. Festivals, celebrations, weddings and even trips to temple are all great opportunities to make (and eat) traditional sweetmeats and mouth-watering goodies.

Many of our puddings involve a grain of some kind – whether it is cracked wheat to be combined with spiced fruit and nuts in *mava lapsi*, or basmati rice in creamy cardamom, almond and pistachio *dhud pak* (rice pudding), or semolina in fragrant almond and sultana *rava no sehro*. Sesame and poppy seeds are regular additions to our sweets and you will often find almonds and pistachios there too, either incorporated into the dish or simply sprinkled on top before serving.

Dairy products like *ghee* and full-fat milk feature heavily, and are used to bring richness to dishes like carrot and cardamom *gajar halva* and sweet cardamom yoghurt *shrikhand*. And of course milk is a vital ingredient in cooling milkshakes too – whether it is pale green avocado and cardamom *roojiraa dhud* or my favourite, bright pink *faludha*, with its fragrant rose flavour, agar agar vermicelli and naughty-but-nice scoop of vanilla ice cream.

If you can't manage a pudding but still fancy a little sugary something to end your meal or to nibble on for elevenses with a cup of hot tea, try irresistible *kopra pak* (Indian coconut fudge) or rich buttery *ghor papdi* (sesame jaggery squares). Or how about a traditional *ladoo*, which can be made with semolina or with broken *bhakri* flatbread – I've included a recipe for each type so that you can experience the different texture and flavour that each one brings.

Finally, no decent Indian cookbook would be complete without a recipe for fruity and delicious mango *lassi* (the ideal partner to chilli-hot dishes, as it refreshes your taste buds and cools you down) and the secret to making the perfect cup of warming, gingery *adhu vari chai*, to be drunk with meals, between meals or simply whenever you feel the need for a nice cup of tea. So, here they are – enjoy!

DRINKS, DESSERTS AND SWEETS

Mango lassi –
Cooling mango yoghurt drink

(WF, OG, N)

A true Indian classic, this rich, refreshing drink is ideal for cooling you down in hot weather or to revive your taste buds when eating chilli-hot food. I use Kesar mango pulp from a tin when making lassi, *partly because sweet, golden, Gujarati-grown Kesar mango – 'the Queen of mangoes' – is the ideal partner for tangy yoghurt, and partly because tinned pulp is wonderfully reliable when you need the fruit to be perfectly ripe and sweet – fresh mangoes can be a bit hit and miss. However, if you'd like to try making this with fresh fruit, just peel, stone and roughly chop a couple of medium Kesar or Alphonso mangoes and use them instead of the tinned pulp.*

SERVES 4

740g plain live set yoghurt
300ml tinned mango pulp
 (ideally Kesar mango)
100g sugar, plus more to taste
8 ice cubes

Blitz all the ingredients in a blender for a couple of minutes until the ice is finely crushed (if you have a hand-held blender, you can do this in a large jug). Taste and add more sugar if you think it needs it.

Cover and refrigerate for at least an hour. When you are ready to serve, give it a good stir and pour into tall glasses to enjoy with your meal. I find that mango *lassi* goes extremely well with rice dishes like *batsai kichdi* (page 160), *biryani* (page 163) and *wattana pilau* (page 169).

Any leftover *lassi* can be covered and kept in the fridge for a couple of days … although in my house there's never any left over.

Roojiraa dhud –
Avocado and cardamom milkshake

(WF, OG, N)

My son Mayur has always been into his drinks – not always non-alcoholic, I might add! I make this for him and he absolutely loves it. It's thick, rich and creamily smooth – delicious and nutritious. Throw a few crushed ice cubes into the blender too if you fancy trying this as an iced smoothie, and feel free to use rice, soya or almond milk instead of whole milk to make a dairy-free version.

SERVES 4

2 small avocados, peeled and destoned

1 litre cold whole milk

70g sugar

1 teaspoon cardamom seeds, coarsely ground or crushed

Roughly chop the avocados, then blitz with the milk and sugar in a blender for a minute or so until thoroughly liquidized (if you have a hand-held blender, you can do this in a large jug). Add the cardamom and give the mixture another quick blitz to combine.

Serve immediately.

VARIATION – KELA DHUD – BANANA CARDAMOM MILKSHAKE

Instead of avocados, use 3 or 4 large ripe bananas and add a handful of crushed ice (or a couple of scoops of vanilla ice cream, if you're feeling indulgent) when blitzing.

VARIATION – CHIKOO DHUD – SWEET SAPODILLA MILKSHAKE

Ripe *chikoo* (or *chico*) fruit has a deliciously sweet flavour, rather like caramelized pear – if you have the opportunity to try it, I recommend that you do!

Omit the cardamom, add a handful of crushed ice (or a few scoops of vanilla ice cream) and blitz the milk and sugar with 4 ripe, peeled and deseeded *chico* fruits instead of avocados for a sweet, malty milkshake treat.

Faludha –
Rose milkshake with ice cream and vermicelli

(WF, OG, N)

Faludha is a lovely refreshing treat that is halfway between a drink and a dessert. In India it is enjoyed at any time of day to help cool off in the phenomenal heat. The soaked basil seeds and agar agar (a type of vegetarian gelatine made from algae) are great for rehydrating and cooling the body, making faludha an excellent drink to enjoy with curry. Do note that the agar agar jelly needs at least 4 hours to cool and set before you can grate it.

SERVES 4

1 teaspoon basil seeds
8g agar agar, cut into 2cm strips
120ml rose syrup,
  plus extra for drizzling
1 litre whole milk
4 scoops of vanilla ice cream

Soak the basil seeds in 300ml of cold water for 10 minutes. Tip into a sieve, leave to drain for 5 minutes, then refrigerate in an airtight container until needed.

Put the agar agar strips and 500ml of warm water into a small pan over a high heat for about 15 minutes, stirring constantly, until the mixture thickens. Pour into a shallow dish or bowl and leave to cool at room temperature for at least 4 hours.

Once the agar agar is set, cut into manageable chunks. Remove from the bowl with a spatula, then carefully grate into long fine strips, like shiny vermicelli.

Divide the syrup, hydrated basil seeds and grated agar agar between 4 tall glasses. Top up with milk, stopping about 3cm from the rim to allow room to add a scoop of ice cream to each glass. Use a long-handled teaspoon to stir, then drizzle the *faludha* with a little extra syrup. Serve straight away, with a wide straw to slurp through and the long-handled teaspoon for scooping up ice cream.

Adhu vari chai –
Ginger-infused tea
(WF, OG, N)

This warming, spicy drink (sometimes called adrak wali chai) *is at the heart and hearth of every Indian home. Each household will have its own way of making it, but the pleasure felt when drinking this soothing tea will be much the same. In India the cups of tea are much smaller than in the UK, but they are drunk much more often . . .*

SERVES 4

7cm root ginger, peeled
 and finely grated
5–6 teaspoons black tea leaves
65g sugar, plus more to taste
600ml whole milk

Put the ginger and 800ml of water into a large pan over a high heat until the water comes to the boil, then stir in the tea leaves and sugar. Bring back to the boil and simmer for 2 minutes, to allow the flavours of the ginger, sugar and tea to combine and work their magic.

Pour in the milk and simmer for 3 minutes over a high heat, stirring occasionally. Keep an eye on the pan and watch out for bubbles forming around the edges (after about 2–3 minutes) – the milky tea can very quickly boil over if you're not careful. The moment it starts to foam up, remove from the heat and blow gently on the surface to cool the tea slightly until it sinks back down.

Reduce the heat to low, return the pan to the heat and leave to simmer for 5 minutes, stirring occasionally. If it stops simmering, briefly increase the heat to bring it back to the boil, then reduce the heat to low again.

Remove from the heat and pour through a tea strainer (or a clean sieve) into cups or mugs.

Serve steaming hot, with extra sugar to add to taste – I think this tea is best drunk with lots of sugar, but then I do have a traditional Gujarati sweet tooth! In our household we drink this with pretty much everything, but it is a particular favourite to accompany snacks like *tikki puri* (page 96) and *aloo gobi paratha* (page 94).

Dhud pak –
Cardamom, almond and pistachio rice pudding

(WF, OG)

Dhud pak is a traditional dessert, usually made in Gujarati homes when we are expecting guests. Interestingly, it is never served at Gujarati wedding feasts as it is considered to be bad luck. This dish requires a close eye to be kept on it, and a lot of stirring, but it is worth it for the smooth, creamy texture of this sweet, cardamom-scented rice pudding. The size of pan you use can help to control the hot milk (the bigger the pan, the less likely it is to boil over) – I use a 24cm diameter, 20cm deep pan, which works really well. Any leftover dhud pak will keep in an airtight container in the fridge for a couple of days – enjoy it cold or, if you prefer, heat it through over a low heat or in the microwave and serve it hot.

SERVES 4

75g basmati rice
2 litres whole milk
100g sugar
½ teaspoon cardamom seeds,
  coarsely ground or crushed
25g pistachios, roughly chopped
55g almonds, roughly chopped

Rinse the rice twice in warm water, then drain.

Heat the milk in a large pan over a high heat for about 3 minutes, stirring all the time, until it starts to steam but not yet boil. This can happen quickly, so keep a close eye on it and keep stirring.

Tip in the rice and continue to stir to circulate the milk so that it doesn't stick and burn, running your spoon across the bottom and sides of the pan. Cook for 18–20 minutes, stirring all the while, until the rice is cooked through. It is important to make sure the rice is fully cooked before you add the sugar, so check that it is soft, with no hardness left at the core of the grain.

Stir in the sugar and cook for a further 1–2 minutes, stirring all the time.

Remove from the heat, sprinkle in the ground cardamom seeds and mix thoroughly, making sure the spice doesn't all clump together. Stir in the pistachios and almonds and leave to rest, uncovered, for at least 15 minutes before serving. I like to eat this warm, but it is delicious cold too.

Shrikhand –
Smooth and creamy cardamom yoghurt

(WF, OG)

This is one of the most important desserts in Gujarati cuisine, and is the must-have dish at a traditional wedding feast. To this day Mohan still compliments Minal's family on the amazing shrikhand *served at her and Bobby's wedding. Traditional* shrikhand *is not a quick dish to make – you need to start preparing it a couple of days before you want to serve it – but its creamily rich texture and sweet, fragrant flavour make it well worth the wait. However, if you're in a hurry, why not try the speedy shortcut version at the end of this recipe? Whichever version you make, any leftovers will keep in an airtight container in the fridge for up to a week – just stir and sprinkle with fresh pistachio slivers before serving.*

SERVES 4

1.7 litres whole milk
95g plain live set yoghurt
215g sugar
1 teaspoon cardamom seeds,
  finely ground
30g pistachios, cut into slivers,
  to finish

Heat the milk in a medium/large ovenproof pan over a high heat and stir until it comes to the boil (this may take 10–15 minutes). Remove from the heat and leave to cool to lukewarm (you want it roughly at body temperature, so test by dipping in a clean finger). It can take 2–3 hours to cool, but you can reduce this time by setting the pan in a sinkful of cold water and stirring frequently to aid the cooling process. Preheat the oven to 110°C/90°C fan/ gas mark ¼.

Stir the yoghurt into the warm milk, then cover the pan and place in the oven. Reduce the temperature to the lowest possible setting (on my oven that's 20°C) and leave overnight to set into a rich yoghurt.

Tip the yoghurt into a clean muslin cloth or bag, tie the top and hang it over the sink (or over a bowl in the fridge) for 6 hours while the whey drips out. Then put the muslin bag into a sieve with a weight on it and leave it to drain again for a further 6 hours to remove any remaining whey.

Scoop the thick curds into a medium bowl and stir in the sugar (the traditional ratio of strained curds to sugar is 4:3, so if you fancy being exact, weigh the strained curds and add 75% of that weight in sugar). Cover the bowl and chill in the fridge for a couple of hours.

Sieve the chilled yoghurt twice to make it smooth and creamy, and to make sure the sugar is evenly distributed. Whisk with an electric beater on a low setting until light and fluffy (this should take about 3–5 minutes), then stir in the ground cardamom seeds.

Cover the bowl again and refrigerate for at least an hour. Sprinkle with pistachios just before serving.

Mix in pomegranate seeds or chunks of fresh mango (or any other fresh fruit that takes your fancy) just before serving.

If you are short of time, try this shortcut method. It won't have quite the same texture as traditional *shrikhand*, but it will still taste delicious.

Leave 800g of plain live set yoghurt in a muslin bag over the sink (or over a bowl in the fridge) to drain for an hour or two. Tip the strained yoghurt into a medium bowl, stir in the sugar, then cover and chill in the fridge for an hour.

Sieve the chilled yoghurt twice, then whisk with an electric beater on a low setting until light and fluffy. Stir in the ground cardamom seeds.

Cover the bowl again and refrigerate for at least an hour. Sprinkle with pistachios just before serving.

Mava lapsi –
Spiced fruit, nut and cracked wheat pudding

(O G)

This Gujarati delicacy is generally cooked during festivals and other celebratory times, although my husband with his sweet tooth would happily eat it every week. As with Christmas pudding, be prepared to feel very full and rather sleepy after enjoying this dish! Do note that broken wheat is not the same as bulgur wheat – bulgur wheat has been steamed before cracking and needs little further cooking, whereas broken or cracked wheat is still raw and needs to be fully cooked. Any leftover mava lapsi *will keep in an airtight container in the fridge for a couple of days – it is wonderful eaten cold, or you can heat it through over a low heat or in the microwave to enjoy it hot again.*

SERVES 4

200g *ghee* (or clarified butter)
200g broken/cracked wheat
4 cardamom pods
4 cloves
6cm cinnamon stick, broken in half
180g sugar
1 teaspoon cardamom seeds,
  coarsely ground or crushed
30g sultanas
15g almonds, cut into slivers
15g pistachios, cut into slivers

Heat the *ghee* in a medium/large pan over a medium heat. Stir in the wheat and gently fry for 7–8 minutes or until light golden brown, stirring occasionally to ensure that it doesn't burn.

Pour in 1.25 litres of boiling water, taking care to stay clear of any sizzling and spitting – I usually put the pan into the sink before adding the water, to avoid covering the hob and myself in buttery spatters!

Return the pan to a medium heat and stir in the cardamom pods, cloves and cinnamon. Simmer three-quarters covered for about 20 minutes, until most of the water has evaporated, checking it every 5 minutes or so and giving it a stir to make sure it doesn't boil dry and burn.

Stir in the sugar and ground cardamom seeds, then cover the pan and leave to cook for 2 minutes. Stir again, then cover the pan again and cook for 10 minutes, stirring every 2–3 minutes. Stir in the sultanas. Cook covered for a further 12–14 minutes or so, still stirring every 2–3 minutes, until the *ghee* starts to separate from the wheat (you'll see the *ghee* collecting around the edges of the pan).

Remove from the heat and sprinkle with the almonds and pistachios. Cover and leave to rest for at least 10 minutes, until the nuts have softened.

Stir to combine, remove the cardamom pods, then tip the *mava lapsi* into a serving bowl and set in pride of place on your table.

Rava no sehro –
Speedy almond and sultana semolina

(OG)

This is a quick, traditional sweet dish, golden and satisfying. It always reminds me of visiting the temple, where it is often served as prashad (a blessed offering). Any leftover sehro *will keep in an airtight container in the fridge for a couple of days – you can eat it cold, but I prefer to heat it through over a low heat or in the microwave.*

SERVES 6

175g *ghee* (or clarified butter)
200g coarse semolina
500ml whole milk
250g sugar
50g sultanas
1 teaspoon cardamom seeds, coarsely ground or crushed
30g almonds, cut into slivers

Melt the *ghee* in medium/large pan over a medium heat. Stir in the semolina and gently fry for about 8–10 minutes, or until lightly browned. Stir continuously while it fries to ensure that it doesn't burn -– and while you stir, enjoy the wonderful buttery scent filling your kitchen!

While the semolina is frying, pour 600ml of boiling water into a medium pan, add the milk and bring to the boil over a medium heat. Remove from the heat.

Once the semolina is browned, carefully pour in the hot milk and water, taking care to stay clear of any sizzling and spitting – I usually put the pan into the sink before I do this.

Return the pan to the heat and simmer uncovered over a low heat for a few minutes or so, until all the liquid has been absorbed. Stir in the sugar and cook gently for a further 3–4 minutes while the semolina thickens, stirring continuously to make sure it doesn't stick or burn.

Stir in the sultanas and ground cardamom seeds, sprinkle with the almonds, then cover the pan and leave to cook for a further 3 minutes. Remove from the heat, stir, then leave to rest, covered, for at least 10 minutes.

Stir again, then tip into a large serving bowl and place at the centre of your feast.

Gajar halva –
Traditional carrot and cardamom pudding

(WF, OG, N)

Ramesh, the sous chef at Prashad, perfected our recipe for this classic Indian pudding with the help of my husband. We once cooked this moist, moreish carrot sweet for more than 1,000 people at a dinner for yoga guru Baba Ramdev, on a remote Scottish island. When Baba Ramdev came to compliment the chefs and extend his blessings, Mohan's smile was enormous, despite twenty-four hours in the kitchens! The milk powder helps to thicken the dish and absorb any excess moisture from the carrots. Any leftover gajar halva *will keep in an airtight container in the fridge for a couple of days – reheat it over a low heat or in the microwave or simply enjoy it cold – it's delicious.*

SERVES 6

240g *ghee* (or clarified butter)

10 medium carrots (approximately 1.15kg), finely grated

500ml whole milk

300g granulated sugar

60g dried milk powder

1¾ teaspoons cardamom seeds, coarsely ground or crushed

30g pistachios, roughly chopped, to finish (optional)

Melt the *ghee* in large thick-based pan over a high heat, then stir in the carrots. Fry for a minute on high, then reduce the heat to medium and cook for about 5 minutes, stirring all the while. Increase the heat to high again and fry for another 4–5 minutes, until the majority of the liquid from the carrots has evaporated. Constant stirring and varying the temperature during frying both help to speed up the process of cooking off the carrot juice.

While the carrots are frying, bring the milk to the boil in a small pan. Once the liquid from the carrots has evaporated, pour in the boiling milk and cook over a high heat for 5 minutes, stirring continuously.

Stir in the sugar and cook for a further 5–6 minutes, stirring regularly to make sure the mixture doesn't stick or burn. Add the milk powder and cardamom and keep stirring and cooking for another 5 minutes, then remove from the heat.

Leave to rest, covered, for at least 30 minutes to allow the flavours to intensify, then gently reheat before serving. The temperature at which you serve the *halva* is a matter of taste – some like it piping hot, while I prefer it slightly warm and accompanied by a scoop or two of good soft vanilla ice cream.

You can serve *gajar halva* in a large bowl, garnished with chopped pistachios if you fancy them (the colour contrast between the green nuts and orange *halva* is lovely). Alternatively you can form it into little domes as I sometimes do, pressing a sixth of the mixture at a time into a small bowl or teacup to mould it into shape, then tipping on to individual serving plates. Sprinkle the tops with chopped pistachios – or, for a real flourish, a twist or two of gold leaf!

Ghor papdi –
Sesame jaggery squares

(OG)

Ghor papdi (also known as gol papdi *or* gur papri*) is an old-fashioned classic Gujarati sweet. During the final of the Gordon Ramsay's Best Restaurant competition, Minal and I made a selection of sweetmeats and Angela Hartnett really loved the texture and richness of this one.*

SERVES 4 (MAKES 16)

115g *ghee* (or clarified butter)
220g chapatti flour
50g sesame seeds
130g jaggery, cut into
 thin flakes (or demerara/
 soft brown sugar)

Melt 85g of the *ghee* in a large frying pan over a medium heat. Add the chapatti flour and keep stirring gently for about 2 minutes, breaking up any lumps, while the flour toasts and darkens slightly. Stir in the sesame seeds and continue to stir for about 5 minutes or so, taking care not to let the flour burn, until the seeds start to pop. Remove from the heat, tip the seed/flour mixture on to a plate and set aside.

Put the remaining 30g of *ghee* and the jaggery into the pan, return to a low heat and stir together as they melt and begin to bubble. Continue to stir for a couple of minutes, making sure nothing sticks or burns, until the jaggery mixture starts to darken, then stir in the seed/flour mixture. Increase the heat to medium and stir for another couple of minutes, then remove from the heat.

Tip the mixture into a 16 x 16cm square tin (at least 2cm deep) and press down to flatten, making sure you push it right to the edges and into the corners. Smooth the top, then use a sharp knife to score it into 16 squares while still warm.

Leave to cool for 15 minutes, then use a spatula to lift the squares carefully out of the tin and on to a plate. Serve while still warm as an afternoon snack or at the end of a meal with a cup of hot *adhu vari chai* (page 228). Once cooled, *ghor papdi* can be stored in an airtight container for up to 3 days, although in our house it never lasts that long …

OPPOSITE – *Ghor papdi* (page 239) and *Soji ladoo* (page 240)

Soji ladoo –
Semolina and white poppy seed sweets
(OG, N)

Literally meaning 'semolina balls', these ladoos *(or laddus) are traditionally prepared to offer at temple as* prashad, *or to celebrate family and religious special occasions.*

SERVES 4 (MAKES 8)

200g *ghee* (or clarified butter)
200g fine semolina
200g plain flour, sieved
sunflower oil, for frying
175g granulated sugar
1½ teaspoons cardamom seeds, coarsely ground or crushed
20g white poppy seeds

Heat 120g of *ghee* in a small pan over a medium heat for a minute or two until melted. Mix the semolina and flour in a bowl. Pour in the melted *ghee* and combine thoroughly. Add 125ml of warm water and use your hands to bring everything together to form a soft dough, then knead for about a minute.

Divide the dough into 8 roughly equal pieces. Hold a piece in your palm, then close your fingers and press them into the centre of the dough. Gently squeeze a few times to shape the *ladoo*, pressing it into your half-closed palm. Repeat with the rest of the dough pieces.

Heat the frying oil – about 25cm deep – in a large pan over a medium heat. Test the temperature by dropping a few little pieces of dough into the oil – when it is hot enough, they will quickly float to the surface. Reduce the heat to low/medium – you want the dough to fry slowly so that it cooks through.

Gently place all the dough pieces in the oil. Using a wooden spoon, move them around so that they cook evenly all over. Fry for 3 minutes, then reduce the heat to low and fry for another 27–28 minutes, turning them every 3–4 minutes, until golden brown and crisp on the outside. Remove from the oil with a slotted spoon and leave to rest on kitchen paper.

Allow to cool for a few minutes, then break the fried dough into little pieces – this will speed up the cooling process and help with crushing them later. Leave to cool for another 10 minutes, or until cold to the touch. Using a wooden spoon, press the pieces through a fine sieve to create equal-sized crumbs (this powdered dough is called *churma*).

Blitz the sugar to a fine texture. Put the sugar and the remaining 80g of *ghee* on a baking tray and use the palm of your hand to work them together in circular motions, grinding the sugar into the *ghee*. Scoop back into a heap and repeat until the mixture is snow-white and very light and airy. This process takes about 8–10 minutes – it's quite a workout, but it's worth it for the great texture it gives to the finished *ladoos*. Add the *churma* and rub the mixture together with your hands, then add the cardamom and mix again.

Form the mixture into 8 balls and flatten them slightly. Put the poppy seeds into a small bowl. Dip half of each *ladoo* in the seeds, then place on a plate, ready to serve with mugs of piping hot *adhu vari chai* (page 228). Any left over will keep in an airtight container for up to a week.

Kopra pak –
Indian coconut fudge

(WF, OG, N)

The festival of raksha bandhan *celebrates the relationship between brothers and sisters. Traditionally sisters tie colourful bands (*rakhi*) on their brothers and feed them homemade sweetmeats, while the brothers dish out expensive presents!* Rakhi *means 'protection', and sisters perform this ritual to protect their brothers for the coming year. My daughter Hina would always make her own special sweetmeats for Bobby and Mayur, and* kopra pak *is one of them.*

SERVES 4 (MAKES 16)

150g sugar
100g dried milk powder
150g unsweetened
  desiccated coconut
1 teaspoon *ghee*
  (or clarified butter)

Put the sugar and 75ml cold water into a medium pan over a medium heat, stirring occasionally. Once the sugar has dissolved, simmer for 2–3 minutes, stirring all the time, then stir in the milk powder and coconut. Reduce the heat to low and continue to stir until the mixture comes together – this will only take a minute or so – then remove from the heat.

Use the *ghee* to grease a 16 x 16cm square tin (at least 2cm deep). Scoop the coconut mixture into the tin and press down to flatten, making sure you push it right to the edges and into the corners. Using a sharp knife, score it into 16 squares while still warm.

Leave to cool for 30 minutes, then use a spatula to lift the squares carefully out of the tin and on to a serving plate. Enjoy with a cup of warming *adhu vari chai* (page 228). Store any leftovers in an airtight container for up to 3 days.

Bhakri ladoo –
Jaggery dough balls

(OG, N)

These substantial sweets, often taken to temple to offer as prashad, are more of a full-blown snack than a dainty nibble. I make these on some of our fasting days to provide plenty of energy during the day. Although these are traditionally made using leftover flatbread, I like to make fresh bhakri *without the usual addition of sugar or oil, as I find that the jaggery and* ghee *in this recipe are enough.*

SERVES 4 (MAKES 8)

400g chapatti flour
145g *ghee* (or clarified butter), plus 30g or so
130g jaggery, cut into thin flakes (or demerara/ soft brown sugar)

To make the *bhakri*, combine the flour and 145g of *ghee* in a large bowl, using your hands to make sure the *ghee* is thoroughly worked in. Pour in 150ml of warm water and mix until the dough starts to come together. Knead for a couple of minutes until firm and smooth.

Divide into 8 roughly equal pieces and form each one into a slightly flattened ball. Place a dough ball on a clean work surface and roll into a disc about 20cm in diameter and roughly 5mm thick (see method on page 91). Repeat with the remaining dough balls, placing the rolled discs on a baking sheet as you go, making sure they don't overlap.

Heat a flat *tawa* pan or a flat-based non-stick frying pan over a very low heat. Dry-fry one of the dough discs in the pan for 6 minutes, turning it every 2 minutes, until you have a crisp, dry-textured flatbread. Remove from the pan and place on a wire rack to cool while you cook the remaining *bhakri*. Leave to cool completely for at least 10 minutes, then break the *bhakri* into small (roughly 3–4mm) pieces over a medium bowl, rubbing them between your palms to help crumble them.

Melt the 30g of *ghee* in a large frying pan over a low heat, then add the jaggery and stir together as the mixture begins to bubble. Continue to stir for a couple of minutes, making sure nothing sticks or burns, until the mixture starts to darken, then remove from the heat and pour on to the *bhakri* pieces. Stir together with a spoon while the mixture cools enough to be handled, then continue to mix using your fingertips. Work the sugary *ghee* into the *bhakri* until all the pieces are thoroughly coated.

Form the mixture into 8 balls with your hands, squeezing tightly to bind them, placing them on a serving plate as you go. If the *ladoos* are crumbly and not binding properly, put them back into the bowl and work another tablespoon of *ghee* through the mixture before trying again.

When we are fasting, we eat these just as they are, but on other occasions I serve them with *dhal* (page 192) and *baath* (page 156) as a sweet, buttery addition to the meal. Any leftovers can be stored in an airtight container for up to 3 days.

OPPOSITE – *Bhakri ladoo* (page 243) and *Kopra pak* (page 241)

MEAL PLANNERS

We all need a little help and inspiration sometimes, particularly when preparing unfamiliar food. Many of us cook only a handful of different meals week in, week out – they're the dishes that we're familiar with, for which we have the ingredients easily to hand, or that we know the family will eat without any drama!

However, it does us all good to change our routine every so often, not least in terms of food. It can be great fun as the cook to prepare something new, with different ingredients and techniques, and it can be equally exciting for the people eating it to try new flavours and maybe even a different vegetable or two.

So I've put together a few suggestions to help introduce my recipes into your cooking. You'll find ideas for:

THREE QUICK MIDWEEK SUPPERS
each with one main dish, one bread
or rice dish and a relish, sauce or dip to go with it.

A WEEKEND DINNER PARTY
a couple of main dishes with rice, bread, *dhal* and a dip, as well as
something sweet to drink and eat (plus there's a starter and accompanying relish
as optional extras, if you are really out to impress).

A SPECIAL OCCASION MENU
to create a fantastic spread, with starter, street snack, main dishes,
lentil-filled bread, rice, soup-sauce, pickles, crunchy salad, relish and
my favourite drink-dessert – in other words, the full Patel family festive feast!

KAUSHY'S TOP TIPS
FOR STRESS-FREE ENTERTAINING

1.

When you are making a big meal for a dinner party or a special occasion,
things can get hectic as you near the time for serving up.
Spread the workload and pick dishes that can be made in advance,
either the day before or on the morning of the dinner party, to be
finished and reheated at the last minute.

2.

You'll find life much easier if you do all the preparation
(washing, trimming, peeling, chopping)
and measure out your ingredients before you start cooking.

3.

Don't worry about everything being piping hot – many dishes are traditionally
served warm or even cold and they taste just as good!

4.

Try to factor in an extra half-hour to clear up in the kitchen,
set the table and get yourself ready, so that you don't feel rushed when cooking
(it affects the flavours and your enjoyment).

These simple steps can help keep stress levels in your kitchen to a minimum,
so that you can enjoy the meal as much as your guests!

QUICK MIDWEEK SUPPERS

Here are three delicious speedy suppers to make in seven simple steps …

SUPPER 1

WATTANA AND FLOWER – PEA AND CAULIFLOWER CURRY
ROTLI – TRADITIONAL PUFFED FLATBREAD
LILA DHANIA LASAN – CORIANDER, CHILLI AND GARLIC RELISH

A lovely meal with fresh, clean flavours – sweetness from the peas, heat from the chillies and a sharp citrus/coriander tang from the relish, perfectly accompanied by soft rotli *bread.*

1. Prepare the *rotli* dough, smooth with oil, cover with clingfilm and leave to rest.
2. Make the *lila dhania lasan* and store in an airtight jar in the fridge.
3. Cook the *wattana* and flower, then sprinkle with coriander, cover and leave to rest.
4. Roll out and cook the *rotli*. Wrap in foil to keep them warm and stop them drying out.
5. Reheat the *wattana* and flower until piping hot.
6. Spoon some *lila dhania lasan* into a small bowl and squeeze lemon juice over it.
7. Serve up with a smile!

SUPPER 2

RENGHAN BATAKA – AUBERGINE AND POTATO CURRY

MUNG DHAL KICHDI – SOOTHING YELLOW LENTIL RICE

KHUDI – SPICED YOGHURT SOUP

Soothing, warming and filling, this meal is perfect for a cold wintry day or a chilly autumn evening, or just whenever you feel the need for a bit of home-cooked comfort food.

1. Prepare the *khudi* and leave to rest, covered.
2. Start the *renghan bataka*. While it is simmering uncovered over a low heat for 5–6 minutes …
3. … get the rice and dhal cooking for the *mung dhal kichdi*.
4. Finish making the *renghan bataka*, cover and set aside to rest.
5. Finish cooking the *mung dhal kichdi*. Once it is also resting …
6. … gently reheat the *khudi*.
7. When the *mung dhal kichdi* is ready, sprinkle the *renghan bataka* with coriander and serve.

SUPPER 3

TARKA DHAL – CURRIED YELLOW AND ORANGE LENTILS

BHAKRI – RUSTIC FLATBREAD

KAKADHI RAITU – COOL CUCUMBER AND YOGHURT DIP

Real Gujarati fast food – traditional spicy lentils with thick, satisfying flatbread and a delicate yoghurt dip. There's a reason these classic dishes have maintained their popularity for so many years, and together they are a winning combination.

1. Start with the *tarka dhal*, and once the pulses are simmering three-quarters covered …
2. … prepare the *bhakri* dough, cover with lightly oiled clingfilm and set aside to rest.
3. Finish cooking the *tarka dhal*, then sprinkle with chopped coriander and leave to rest, covered.
4. Make the *raitu*, spoon into a serving bowl, then cover and refrigerate until needed.
5. Roll out and fry the *bhakri* and wrap in foil to keep them warm.
6. Reheat the *tarka dhal* until piping hot.
7. Stir the chilled *raitu* and serve with plenty of hot *tarka dhal* and warm *bhakri*. Enjoy!

WEEKEND DINNER PARTY

PETHIS – **GARLIC-COCONUT FILLED POTATO BALLS (OPTIONAL)**
RENGHAN LILVA – **AUBERGINE AND INDIAN BROAD BEAN CURRY**
SUKHU BHINDA BATAKA – **MUSTARD SEED, OKRA AND POTATO CURRY**
BAATH – BOILED BASMATI RICE
PURI – FRIED PUFFY BREAD
DHAL – **TRADITIONAL YELLOW LENTIL SOUP**
METHI SAFARJAN – FENUGREEK, CHILLI AND APPLE RELISH (OPTIONAL)
KANDHA RAITU – ONION AND YOGHURT DIP
MANGO LASSI – **COOLING MANGO YOGHURT DRINK**
RAVA NO SEHRO – **SPEEDY ALMOND AND SULTANA SEMOLINA**

I cooked this meal for my daughter Hina and her husband Bhavesh when they last came to visit from Chicago (Bhavesh loves my food, and I love cooking it for him). If this is the first time you have prepared a big multi-dish Indian meal, you may wish to leave out the pethis *and* methi safarjan *– there'll still be plenty of variety in flavours and textures with two delicious curries, refreshing* raitu, *spicy* dhal, *fluffy steamed rice,* puri *bread, fruity* lassi *and sweet golden* rava no sehro.

THE DAY BEFORE – EVENING

1. Make the *lassi,* cover and store in the fridge.
2. Prepare the *methi safarjan* (if making) and place in an airtight container in the fridge. Making it in advance allows the spices to infuse and the apple chunks to soften.
3. Follow the recipe for *pethis* (if making) until all the coconut balls have been wrapped in potato casing, then place on a plate or tray, cover with clingfilm and refrigerate. Don't make them any earlier than the day before the dinner, otherwise the moisture from the coconut will soften the casing and cause problems when frying.
4. Wash, dry and cut up the okra, spread the pieces on a baking tray and leave to oxidize.

(If this is the first time you've cooked a big multi-course Indian meal, allow about 3½–4 hours.)

5. Start with the *dhal*, and once the lentils are simmering three-quarters covered …

6. … cook the *renghan lilva* and set aside to rest, covered.

7. Make the *sukhu bhinda bataka* and leave it to rest, covered, too.

8. Prepare the *puri* dough, cover with lightly oiled clingfilm and set aside to rest.

9. Finish cooking the *dhal*, then leave to rest, covered, while the flavours develop.

10. Roll out and fry the *puri*, then place in a large serving bowl. While *puri* are undeniably delicious eaten hot and crispy straight from the pan, this just isn't practical when you are preparing a large dinner. In any event, they are traditionally eaten lukewarm or cold, so don't worry about trying to keep them hot.

11. Make the *raitu*, spoon into a serving bowl, cover and refrigerate until needed.

12. Start preparing the *rava no sehro*, and once the semolina is frying in the *ghee* …

13. … rinse the rice and start cooking the *baath*.

14. Cook the *sehro* and *baath* side by side (the timings work well), then leave both to rest.

15. If you are making *pethis*, check the casing for cracks, nipping together any you find, then re-roll in a smooth ball between your palms. Fry in the oil the *puri* were fried in (or oven-bake if you want a healthier option). Leave to drain on kitchen paper, then place in a serving dish.

ABOUT 5 MINUTES BEFORE SERVING

16. Spoon the *methi safarjan* (if serving) into a dish.

17. Reheat the rested *renghan lilva*, *sukhu bhinda bataka* and *dhal*. Transfer to serving dishes.

18. Stir the *rava no sehro* and tip into a large serving bowl.

19. Remove the foil from the *baath*, gently run a spoon through and tip into a serving dish.

20. Uncover the *raitu* and give it a good stir.

21. Stir the *lassi* and pour into tall glasses.

SERVICE!

22. In Gujarati cuisine we serve all the dishes at the same time, so put everything on the table for people to help themselves to whatever they fancy.

23. Traditionally the ladies of the household serve the menfolk, but it's really not necessary. So come on boys, serve yourselves — and don't forget to clear the table afterwards and do the washing up!

SPECIAL OCCASION FEAST

WATTANA NI KACHORI – SPICED PEA AND GARLIC CHAPATTI BALLS
KAMREE – **SAVOURY LENTIL PORRIDGE**
RENGHAN REVEYA – **ROUND AUBERGINE SATAY**
BOMBAY BATAKA – **TAMARIND, TOMATO AND POTATO CURRY**
WATTANA PILAU – FRESH PEAS AND RICE
VELMI – SWEET AND BUTTERY LENTIL-FILLED FLATBREAD
KHUDI – SPICED YOGHURT SOUP
RAI MARCHA – PICKLED GREEN CHILLIES WITH MUSTARD SEEDS
SAMBHARO – CHILLI, CARROT, CABBAGE AND PEPPER SALAD
SHIMLA MIRCH – RED PEPPER AND CARROT RELISH
FALUDHA – ROSE MILKSHAKE WITH ICE CREAM AND VERMICELLI

To celebrate our twenty-fifth wedding anniversary, Mohan gave me a beautiful pearl necklace and we invited some close friends round for this meal. There is the most wonderful variety in textures, flavours, colours, aromas and even temperatures (with hot, warm and cold dishes) in this menu – it is a true celebration of amazing Gujarati food!

THE DAY BEFORE – MORNING

1. Rinse the *chana dhal* for the *kamree*, then leave it and the *magaj* flour to soak.
2. Prepare the agar agar for the *faludha* and leave to set.
3. Make the *rai marcha* and leave to marinate in an airtight container in the fridge.

THE DAY BEFORE – EVENING

4. Drain and grind the *chana dhal*. Mix with the *magaj* flour, *masala*, coriander, salt and turmeric. Store this *kamree* mix in an airtight container in the fridge until needed.
5. Soak and drain the basil seeds for the *faludha*, then refrigerate in an airtight container.
6. Grate the agar agar into thin vermicelli strips. Keep in an airtight container in the fridge.
7. Make the *shimla mirch* relish, spoon into an airtight container and refrigerate until needed (I make extra to serve with that evening's meal too, as it goes with so many dishes).
8. Follow the recipe for *wattana ni kachori* until all the filling balls have been wrapped in dough and placed on a lightly oiled tray, then cover with clingfilm and refrigerate.

(If this is the first time you've cooked a big multi-course Indian meal, allow about 4½–5 hours.)

9. Make the *sambharo*, tip into a serving bowl, cover and leave at room temperature.

10. Boil the potatoes for the Bombay *bataka* (set a timer so that they don't overcook).

11. Prepare the sweet *dhal* for the *velmi*, and while it is cooling …

12. … peel and cube the potatoes for the Bombay *bataka* and set aside.

13. Cook the *kamree* and leave to rest, cool and thicken uncovered. I serve this cold as a delicious contrast to the hot food, but you can warm it through before serving if you prefer.

14. Make the *renghan reveya* and set aside to rest, covered.

15. Prepare the *khudi*, leave to rest and cool for 10 minutes, then refrigerate until needed.

16. Cook the Bombay *bataka*, cover and leave to rest while the flavours infuse.

17. Make the *wattana pilau* and leave it to rest too.

18. Check the *wattana ni kachori* dough casing for cracks, nipping together any you find, then re-roll into smooth balls between your palms and fry (or oven-bake). Leave to rest on kitchen paper, then place in a serving dish.

19. Roll the cooled *dhal* into balls, prepare the dough and finish making the *velmi*.

ABOUT 5 MINUTES BEFORE SERVING

20. Spoon the *shimla mirch* and *rai mircha* into little serving bowls or dishes.

21. Warm the *kamree* through, if you don't want to serve it cold.

22. Reheat the rested *renghan reveya*, Bombay *bataka* and *khudi* and transfer to serving dishes.

23. Gently run a spoon through the *wattana pilau* and tip into a serving dish.

24. Toss the *sambharo* delicately to mix together.

WHILE EVERYONE IS HELPING TO CARRY ALL THE DISHES TO THE DINING TABLE

25. Heat through the *ghee* for the *velmi*.

26. Make the *faludha* and serve straight away before the ice cream melts.

AND FINALLY …

27. Get the party started!

Kaushy's
store cupboard and supplies

I am very lucky that I can buy all my fresh Indian vegetables, spices and supplies in local supermarkets in Bradford. If you have an Indian store nearby, ask them to help you with sourcing ingredients (and maybe a traditional masala dabba *spice tin) – even if they don't sell what you're looking for, they should know where you can get hold of it. Many supermarkets now stock a good range of Indian food products and there are plenty of online suppliers too, such as* www.itadka.com, www.spicesofindia.co.uk, www.asiangrocersonline.co.uk, www.theasiancookshop.co.uk, www.asianstoreuk.co.uk *and* www.indianmart.co.uk, *so between the high street and the internet you should be able to find what you need.*

You can buy my secret-blend garam masala *via our website, and if it's cooking equipment you're after, why not get yourself set up with one of my kitchen utensil kits (also available through* www.prashad.co.uk)? *With* rotli *tongs,* bhaat *rice serving spoon, long-handled ladle, whisk, slotted spoon for frying, sturdy rolling pin, ginger grater, small tea strainer and trusty wooden spoon at the ready, you'll be cooking up a fabulous feast in no time!*

To help you achieve that authentic Prashad flavour,
here are some of my favourite brands:

ASLI ATTA
medium chapatti flour

COLMAN'S
fresh garden mint sauce

COFRESH
sev
sev momra/mamra

DESI
paneer

EAST END
almonds, cashews and pistachios
chana dhal/dal
green cardamom pods
masoor dhal/dal
mung dhal/dal
medium red chilli powder
sesame seeds
tinned chickpeas in brine
urad dhal/urid dal

ENO
fruit salts

HEERA
lemon juice
dried milk powder
cooking salt

HEINZ
white vinegar

KHOLAPURI
jaggery

LAKES
pure butter *ghee*

JAIPUR
magaj flour
sorghum flour

KTC
kala chana (desi chana) tinned brown
chickpeas in salted water

NATCO
cracked wheat
fenugreek seeds and dried
fenugreek leaves
kesar mango pulp, tinned
magaj flour
pauwa flattened rice
red chillies, dried
rock salt
semolina, fine and coarse
tamarind slab
white poppy seeds

PAPA
gram (chickpea) flour

PEACOCK
agar agar
rice flour

SUGAM
paneer

TATE & LYLE
granulated sugar

TILDA
basmati rice

TRS
Malawi/tuvar/toor dhal

VANDEVI
asafetida

VB & SONS
cracked wheat

WHITE PEARL
broken rice

ACKNOWLEDGEMENTS

Remembering my God, and in particular the holy sages Shri Gurudev Datta and Dada Bhagavan, I would like to thank you for the energy and motivation you have given me to write this cookbook.

I would also like to thank my parents for bringing me into this world and for ensuring that my childhood was enriched with my grandmother's love and her infectious energy for cooking. Special thanks to my mother, Shanta Bha, for believing in me, and to my grandmother, Prem Ma, for imparting all her wonderful qualities, nurturing my confidence and lovingly showing me the enjoyment of cooking.

I am so grateful to my husband, Mohan, for always encouraging and supporting me, in particular during the early years when he afforded me the luxurious housewife life that enabled me to develop my recipes and enrich my children with love through my food. He is my rock. It is his belief and confidence in me that has brought me out of my shell and allowed me to shine.

Thank you to Gordon Ramsay for coming into our lives, for his heartfelt and loving guidance, for offering Minal training at Petrus and for giving me direction and encouragement to write this book.

I would like to thank my son Bobby for his encouragement, belief and continual support during the writing of the book. We have been on a wonderful journey together and without him it would never have been completed. I am very pleased that during this time we have become even closer and he has been able to understand my life.

I am extremely proud that this journey has helped me to impress and excite my 'babies', my daughter Hina and son Mayur. I am so grateful for all the support they have given me during the whole process, through tasting, recipe ideas and making sure I had everything I needed.

I am very grateful to my daughter-in-law Minal, who is actually like a daughter to me, for taking on the successful running of Prashad and thus allowing me the time to concentrate on writing. She also made sure I always had all the ingredients necessary for each recipe, leaving me to focus on cooking.

I would like to thank my entire team at Prashad, in particular restaurant manager Mohamed Imran Shaukat and sous chef Rameshkumar Rajpuruhit, for their endless energy and passion for perfection, their honest feedback on recipe tasting and their unshakeable commitment to ensuring that Prashad is always the very best it can be. And obviously a huge thank you to all our customers (past and present) for supporting us, loving our food and nominating Prashad for the Best Restaurant competition.

Thank you to my agents, Alexandra Henderson and Annabel Merullo, for seeing my potential, for persisting in winning our confidence and for hosting a tasting day in London from which my relationship with Hodder and Saltyard Books began. I am grateful to my publisher, Elizabeth Hallett, for her charming, calming influence throughout the process of creating this book. I would like to thank my lovely editor Bryony Nowell for her wonderful way with words, her great encouragement, her tactful eye for detail and her patience. She has ensured that my words come to life and has really encapsulated my warmth, love and energy in every single recipe.

Thank you to Ali, Ami, Sparky and the other volunteer recipe testers who have provided such helpful feedback, and to Kate, Claudette, Emma, Bea, James and everyone else at Saltyard Books who played a part in making this beautiful book.

Thank you to everyone at the Cooking School at Dean Clough – teaching my cooking there gives me so much pleasure.

Most of all, I am thankful for the magical gift that my grandma ignited within me, and so grateful that through this love and passion I now spend my time teaching cooking courses and exploring other amazing opportunities to share my culinary world.

There are many more people who have been involved with making this book and I would like to thank each and every one who has helped make this a really enjoyable and laughter-filled experience. My love is now in written form, for which I want to say *Thank You*.

INDEX

Page references for photographs are in **bold**

First published in Great Britain in 2012 by Saltyard Books
An imprint of Hodder & Stoughton
An Hachette UK company

3

Copyright © Kaushy Patel, 2012
Photography © Cristian Barnett, 2012

A CIP catalogue record for this title is available from the British Library.

ISBN 978 1 444 73471 3

Typeset in Sabon and Nexus
Design by www.cabinlondon.co.uk
Food stylist Sunil Vijayakar
Props stylists Morag Farquhar and Kasha Harmer
Project editor Bryony Nowell
Copy editor Annie Lee
Proof reader Margaret Gilbey
Indexer Caroline Wilding

Printed and bound in England by Butler Tanner & Dennis

Hodder & Stoughton policy is to use papers that are natural, renewable and recyclable products and made from wood grown in sustainable forests. The logging and manufacturing processes are expected to conform to the environmental regulations of the country of origin.

Hodder & Stoughton Ltd
338 Euston Road
London NW1 3BH

WWW.SALTYARDBOOKS.CO.UK